JAK

MW01717293

COLOGNE

BONECHI

Deutsche Auslieferung:
Paulsen Buchimport / d.i.v.a.
Rosenau 16
79618 Rheinfelden
fon: (+49)(0)7623-3097694
fax: (+49)(0)7623-3097696
mail: bonechi@paulsen-buchimport.com
www.paulsen-buchimport.com
ISBN 978-3-944027-01-2

Project and design: *Casa Editrice Bonechi*
Editorial management: *Monica Bonechi*
Picture research: *Marco Bonechi*
Graphic design and cover: *Alessandro Calonego*
Layout: *Patrizia Fabbri*
Texts by *Jakob Schlafke*; *Patrizia Fabbri*, *Giulia Fonnesu* and *Hajo Paulsen*
Editing and updated texts: *Patrizia Fabbri*, *Hajo Paulsen*
Drawing and map (inside covers): *Stefano Benini*

© Copyright 2013
by Casa Editrice Bonechi
Via Cairoli 18/b
Florence - Italy
E-mail: bonechi@bonechi.it

Collective work. All rights reserved.
No part of this publication may be reproduced, stored, or transmitted in any form or by any means, whether electronic, chemical, or mechanical, by photocopying or by any other system including radio, television, or by any information storage and retrieval system, without the express written permission of the publisher.

The cover and layout of this publication are the work of *Casa Editrice Bonechi* graphic artists and as such they are protected by international copyright.

Printed in Italy by *Centro Stampa Editoriale Bonechi*.

The photographs belong to the Archives of *Casa Editrice Bonechi* and were taken by *Marco Bonechi*.

Other contributors:
Corbis: photographs page 71; *Marka*: photographs pages 3 (© Friedrich), 16/17 (© Werner Dieterich), 19 (© Petr Zurek), 21 above left (© Walter G. Allgöwer), 22 above (© Michael Leonhard) and below (© Artcolor); *SIE/Simephoto*: photographs page 30 below (© Lubenow Sabine/SIME-4Corners Images) and cover (© Gräfenhain Günter/SIME-4Corners Images).

The publisher apologies for any omissions and is willing to make amends on being informed by the holders of rights.

ISBN 978-88-476-2728-4

www. bonechi.com

* * *

A 10 9 8 7 6 5 4 3 2 1

A dramatic photograph of the centre of Cologne as it was at the end of the war, devastated by Allied bombing, in the spring of 1945: the Cathedral can be recognized and what remained of the bridge over the Rhine.

Historical Outline

Talking about Cologne means examining two thousand years of history. While work was in progress on the building of the underground in the area of the Cathedral and the station, archaeologists brought to light numerous finds which were on display to the public at the "Rom am Dom" exhibition of 1970. Today we have precise information on the Roman period. We know, for example, that Agrippa, as Governor of Gaul, transferred the town of the Ubii from the right bank to the left bank of the Rhine: the Rhine boundary thus guaranteed a certain protection. The year 38 BC marks the founding of the settlement of the Ubii and its temple, Ara Ubiorum, *in the vicinity of which was a camp of legionaries. In 9 AD, Arminius's crushing defeat of Varus, whose army of two thousand men was annihilated in the battle of the Teutoburg forest, had far-reaching consequences on the town of the Ubii. When the Emperor Tiberius came to power in 14 AD, Cologne was a summer camp for four legions and a winter camp for the 1st and 20th legions. The 6th of November 15 AD is the birth date of Agrippina, daughter of Germanicus and mother of the Emperor Nero. She saw to it that her town of birth became a Roman colony by rank and law, which was to be called Colonia Claudia Ara Agrippinensium. And that is how Cologne's history started. In 70 the town walls were completed and in 90 it became the capital of southern Germany. In 98 the Emperor Trajan, at that time stationed in Cologne, succeeded the Emperor Nerva and the town benefited from about 150 years of development and peace.*

The town of Cologne, which covered an area of almost 100 hectares and was protected against floods, boasted 20,000 inhabitants. In front of it, on the Rhine, was an island almost one kilometer long. Industry and trade prospered. Alongside other religions, such as the worship of Mithras, Christianity spread. On the site where the Cathedral now stands, evidence was found of the first archipiscopal church. The first known bishop, Maternus, took part in the synod of Rome and Arles in 313/314. In 284 Emperor Diocletian divided the Empire into new administrative districts and asked the soldiers for a sacrifice to the gods, but the martyrs of the legion of Thebes resisted the emperor's orders. In 310 Constantine, Emperor of Gaul from 306, built in Cologne the first fixed bridge over the Rhine and consolidated the bridgehead on the right of the Rhine through the Castle of Deutz. In 312 he engaged in war for the domination of the Empire, and after his victory at the Milvian Bridge in 313 he sent the Christians in Milan the edict on the freedom of worship.

Nonetheless, the danger of an attack on the part of migratory peoples still existed. In 355 the Salian Franks attacked the town of Cologne, occupying it for ten months, until Julian the Apostate reconquered it in 356. Difficult years followed for the Christians. In 388, Cologne was once again conquered and sacked by the Franks. In 397, Severinus became bishop of Cologne: in practice, Roman rule came to an end in 401, when Stilicho led the legions to Italy on a military campaign. The safety of the Rhine frontier was in the hands of the Franks, whose Ripuarian branch conquered Cologne and made it the capital in 455. In 496 King Clovis, following his victory over the Alemanni, had himself baptized: that is how the Christianization of the Franks began.

1959 marked the discovery inside the atrium of the city's first Cathedral of a small Chapel dedicated to our Lady and containing the tombs of a woman and child of the house of King Theudebert II, who had been buried there together with precious grave goods in 550.

The following two hundred years were characterized by bitter power struggles, which were concluded by Carolingian rule and the reign of Charlemagne, who was crowned Emperor in Rome in 800. His friend and councillor, the bishop Hildebold of Cologne, in 795 was appointed archbishop of a new, larger ecclesiastic province that extended from Hamburg to Belgium. In 818 he had the old Cathedral demolished and a new, monumental one, which was consecrated in 870, built. In this period there were also six convents of monks and nuns, which included St. Gereon, the most important church, dating back to the 4th century, which due to its wall mosaics was called "to the golden Saints". In 689 Pepin the Younger, together with his wife Plectrude, had the important monastery of St. Maria im Kapitol built on the site of the original Roman capitoline temple.

Cologne's city coat-of-arms, distinguished by three crowns, representing the Three Kings, and eleven drops of blood in memory of the legendary 11,000 virgins of Saint Ursula, who was martyred in Cologne.

In 881 the city that was then flourishing was conquered and sacked by the Normans, who had reascended the Rhine, and took a long time to recover.

With Archbishop Bruno (953-965), the younger brother of Emperor Otto, who in 953 was at the same time Archbishop of Cologne and Grand Duke of Lorraine, the glorious period of the city's history commenced, which even today is reflected in the magnificence of its Romanesque churches. Cologne was ruled by archbishops until 1288. With the extension of the walls to the Rhine, Bruno extended the protected town area to 125 hectares. The city walls were lengthened once again in 1106, and again in 1180, so that Cologne, with its 40,000 inhabitants, was the most highly populated German city and had the longest city walls.

The most noteworthy archbishops to succeed Bruno were: Gero, who was sent by Otto I to Byzantium to ask the hand of Princess Theophanu on behalf of the Emperor, and who is remembered by the imposing Cross of Gero *in Cologne Cathedral; Heribert (999-1021), according to whose will the Chancellor Otto III, his friend, built the Monastery of Mary at Deutz, the present St. Heribert. Under his successor Pilgrim (1021-1036), the Chancellorship for the Italian provinces was connected to the Archbishopric of Cologne in 1031. During the same period, the archbishops also obtained the right to be crowned in Aachen. Pilgrim's successor, Hermann II (1036-1056) of the Ezzo family, operated even in Poland at the Abbey of Tyniec, founded by Brauweiler near Kracow. The year 1049 marked Pope Leo IX's visit. At the time, the Pope and the Emperor were honorary members of the Cathedral Chapter in Cologne, an ecclesiastic honour, remembered by Pope John Paul II during his second visit to Cologne on 15 November 1980. Hermann II also had the first coins minted with the inscription "Sacra Colonia", an honorary title that the town continued to hold in later years. The number of large monasteries and abbeys rose to fourteen: apart from the Cathedral, there were St. Andreas, St. Aposteln, St. Cecilia's, St. Georg, St. Gereon, St. Kunibert, St. Maria im Kapitol, St. Maria Lyskirchen, Great St. Martin, St. Pantaleon, St. Severin, St. Ursula and St. Heribert in Deutz.*

In the 11th century (1056-1075), Hermann's successor, Anno, continued the line of great archbishops. His contemporaries sang his praises, calling him the "flower and light of Germany", whereas as a matter of fact there was growing discontent on the part of some town-dwellers who were becoming increasingly conscious of their rights.

A very important year in the history

of Germany is 1164, marking the arrival in the city of the bones of the Three Kings, which Emperor Frederick Barbarossa sent as precious spoils of war to the Archbishop of Cologne and his Chancellor, Rainald of Dassel, after the conquest of Milan in 1162. The reliquary of the Three Kings was to have no equal in the world. The work, started in 1180 by Nicholas of Verdun, was completed during the following fifty years and Cologne became one of the most important destinations for Christian pilgrims.

The Reliquary of the Three Kings *was finished under the rule of Archbishop Engelbert (1216-1225), who came to power under Emperor Frederick II Hohenstaufen in 1221. A lover of justice and a strong, energetic man, he carried out a decisive role in the politics of the Empire.*

Long-lasting evidence of the strength and power of that century is provided by the Cathedral, which was started in 1248. But when the chancel was completed in 1322, the archbishops no longer ruled the city. In fact, on 5 June 1288, in a battle near Worringen the townsfolk broke the territorial rule of the archbishops, whose prestige and greatness is remembered with recognition in our own age in the "Year of the Romanesque church".

The power of the people during this period can be seen today in the Overstolzen House on the Rheingasse, dating from the 13th century. Its name keeps alive the memory of one of the families which played a decisive role in the struggles between the archbishops and townsfolk who, thanks to trade, became rich and powerful. In 1106 Henry IV granted the townsfolk the right to defend their city. In 1180, the city walls were extended to five and a half kilometres: Cologne was the largest city in the Empire. 150 churches and chapels stood out on the city's skyline; art and science flourished. The studii generali of the Dominicans and Franciscans, with teachers such as Albertus Magnus, Eckhart, Tauler and Duns Scotus, made Cologne a stronghold of science on a European scale.

But civil strife continued. In the 14th century the families clashed with the guilds for domination of the city. In 1396 the coalition act was the first democratic statute to completely eliminate class differences. It was the result of the victory of the guilds over the aristocrats; a symbol of this victory is the tower of the City Hall which was built at the beginning of the 15th century. From then onwards the highest authority was the Council, which as a central organ consisting of 49 members, was elected by the "Gaffeln", the craftsmens' guilds.

In Cologne, the word Hansa also brings to mind an old tradition; it

Simon Meister (1796-1844) (attr.), *The Carnival of Cologne of 1836*, 1836. Cologne, City History Museum.

pursued mainly economic goals. In 1367 the cities of the confederation of Cologne joined in combat against King Valdemar IV Atterdag, who in 1361 had taken possession of the island of Gotland and destroyed the Hansa's fleet. Amongst other things, they conquered Copenhagen and in 1370, with the peace of Stralsund, they obtained the guarantee of their supremacy in trade. The room in the City Hall of Cologne where the alliance took place is even today called the Hanseatic Hall.

Also in the field of science, the inhabitants of Cologne proved their worth. Even though the city had an old tradition of universities founded by various orders, 1388 marks the foundation of the first state university in Germany. In 1475 Emperor Frederick III formally declared Cologne to be a free city of the Empire, thus sealing the evolution started far back in 1288. An image of the town as it was in about 1500 is preserved in an engraving by Anton Woensam.

The tumults of the Reformation period left very little space for building projects. The City Hall was enlarged, while works on the Cathedral, which was still an impressive building, were suspended in 1560 until 1842, when work was resumed with enthusiasm. At the beginning of the 17th century the shipyards were built. Among the most significant buildings to remember is the Jesuit Monastery with the Mariä Himmelfahrtskirche built by Christoph Wämser between 1618 and 1627. During the Thirty Years' War (1618-1648), the part of the city on the east bank of the Rhine was saved, but it was still affected by this period of poverty and famine.

The Dutch influence is to be noted in all the buildings constructed between the end of the 17th and the beginning of the 18th century. Baroque dominated the decorations of interiors and precious altar furnishings and cult objects were mainly created by artists of southern Germany.

After the difficult years of the 17th century and the Spanish Wars of Succession (1701-1714), the cultural and artistic revival was suddently interrupted by the French Revolution. In 1794 Cologne was occupied, and in 1801 it was annexed to France. It marked the end of the free city of the Empire and the Kur-Cologne Archmonastery. In 1796 the Cathedral and numerous churches were desecrated; the Mariä Himmelfahrtskirche became the Temple of Reason, monasteries were closed and church property disappeared. But some art lovers with initiative managed to save part of the artistic wealth of the Church; the name, Franz Ferdinand Wallraf (1748-1824), stands out among these.

In 1815, Cologne was handed over to Prussia and once again became a vital point of trade and industry. In 1822 the bridge over the Rhine was inaugurated, followed in 1859 by the first fixed bridge connecting roads and railways. As from 1883, new towns were annexed with the result that Cologne counted one million inhabitants in 1980. In 1881 the medieval walls were closed and a new wall enclosure was built. After the First World War Konrad Adenauer, mayor of Cologne from 1917 to 1933 and the first Federal Chancellor in 1949, enclosed the city with a green ring, a large public park.

During the Second World War, bombs destroyed 78% of the city and as much as 90% of the old part. The Cathedral with its high towers rose in the middle of the rubble. For the seven hundredth anniversary of the foundation of the Cathedral, the Cardinal of Cologne Frings invited Pope Pius XII together with the main bishops and cardinals of the states which were originally hostile, as a token gesture of reconciliation and affection of old Christian Europe and the beginning of new, peaceful development.

Cologne during Roman Times

In the winter of 1969-1970, an exhibition entitled "Rom am Dom", displaying part of the treasures brought to light during the building of the underground, was held. In 1941, during the building of an air-raid shelter near the Cathedral, the *Dionysus Mosaic* was discovered six metres below ground level. In 1946, after the war, it was displayed to the public in a small museum. On 15 August 1948, during the seven hundredth anniversary of the laying of the Cathedral's foundation stone, the mosaic, having been kept in an alcohol bath for two weeks, was unveiled in all its splendour. Being evidence that the Cathedral already existed in the 3rd century, it would be the most interesting piece in the **Roman-Germanic Museum**, completed in 1974.
In May 1946 Professor Doppelfeld, appointed by the Cathedral Chapter, began excavations under the church, which led to the discovery of the Carolingian Episcopal Church and a Roman temple dating from the 1st century AD. In 1969, near the house where the *Dionysus Mosaic* was found, a room dedicated to Mithras was brought to light, one of the three discovered in Cologne showing that the worship of Mithras was widespread especially during the 3rd century. Not only do the precious finds discovered near the Cathedral and now displayed in the Museum date back to the Roman period: the excavations carried out under the City Hall also led to the discovery of finds dating back to that era. In fact, discoveries were made of the remains of four Praetorian buildings which were erected one after another as the residence of the head of the town for the Southern German Province. As far back as 1570 the Senator Hermann von Weinsberg, during the construction of the new City Hall, examined the impressive walls, making a note of it in his diary. But more in-depth research was possible only after 1953, following the destruction caused by bombings during the last war. A representative palace was found, together with the Aula Regia, where judiciary debates were held. The foundation of the four praetorian buildings can be dated back to the first four centuries AD.
1830 marked the discovery near the Praetorium of

The *Sepulcher of Poblicius* (ca. 50 AD), rising to a height of almost 15 metres, today at the Roman-Germanic Museum.

the opening of a section of sewer pipe 140 metres long, 1.2 metres wide and 2-2.5 metres high, through which the Romans channelled waste water into the Rhine as early as about the middle of the 1st century.
In other parts, discoveries were made of channels of the network that distributed water from the Eifel to homes in Cologne by means of a Roman aqueduct over 90 kilometres long. When the Romans left Cologne in the 5th century, the aqueduct was neglected and no longer of any use, to the extent that in the 11th century the inhabitants of the area used its remains as building material.
The most impressive findings of the Roman era are the town walls, one of the largest transalpine fortifications. In 50 AD building commenced on defence bastions: the embattled walls four kilometres long and at least 7.8 metres high were encircled by a moat 9 metres wide and 3-4 metres deep. Construction was completed in 70, during the revolt of the Batavi. Of the new gates, three face eastwards overlooking the Rhine, three westwards, two are south-facing while the remaining one is north-facing. The side entrance of the latter, referred to in the Gospel as the "eye of the needle" can be seen from the top of the Cathedral. Inside the walls are 19 round towers with a diameter of 9.2 metres. One gets an idea of what the building looked like by starting from the Cathedral and covering a kilometre in a westwards direction until one reaches the tower on the corner, the "Roman tower".
The part of the town most protected from floods was an island, 180 metres wide, facing the east side of the walls. In the centre of it rose a building, 71.5 metres wide and 76 metres long, just to the right of the Praetorium. In the eastern

The Roman-Germanic Archaeological Museum of Cologne is today housed in the large building erected in 1974 next to the Cathedral on the site of a large Roman villa, the place where the now celebrated mosaic with scenes from the life of Dionysus was discovered (ca. 220 AD). Today it is the mosaic which forms the superb floor of the museum, where lavish collections of art works and objects of everyday use are exhibited, illustrating the culture and splendour of Roman and early medieval Cologne.

part was a basin measuring 34 by 17.2 metres and with a depth of 1.55 metres, covered in tufo tiles and with a tiled edge 5 metres wide. Ceramic fragments dating back to the first half of the 1st century AD were found in the square and basin and the construction dates back to a period in which Cologne was no longer part of

Above, a detail of the magnificent *Dionysus Mosaic*; right, a view of the collection of terracottas and glass objects from the Roman age, the largest in the world.

Left, the tombstone of Caius Messulenus, a freed slave who had taken the name of the master to whom he owed his freedom.

The striking presentation of exhibits in one of the rooms of the museum, with (above) what remains of a Hellenistic group of the 3rd century representing children playing piggyback.

a Roman province. Gerta Wolff, to whom we owe the best guide of Roman-Germanic Cologne, goes farther than the simple explanation that it was a sports area and suggests that the sacred area of the *Ara Ubiorum*, which has not yet been discovered, may have been located here.

In the 2nd century the Romans built spacious vestibules on the island, including Vestibule C, which could be the building that was later replaced by the present church of Great St. Martin. Access is gained to the island also through the bridge built in 310 by Constantine, as Emperor of Gaul, to reach the Castle of Deutz, built by him. Nowadays it is no longer possible to distinguish the island because Archbishop Bruno (953-965) had the arm of the Rhine that separated it from the town walls reclaimed and, by building new fortifications, he included it in the urban area, which then passed from 100 to 125 hectares.

In one of the most important archaeological areas of Cologne is the Roman governor's palace, situated below the modern City Hall. This was the site of the administrative centre of the Southern Germanic Province, whose head or "propraetor" was usually an ex-consul. As representative of the emperor, he was commander-in-chief of the troops stationed in the province and exercized his authority over civil administration, justice and the police force; he was also responsible for the cult of the emperor. Apart from the bureaucratic apparatus of the provincial administration, 500 mounted soldiers and 500 foot-soldiers depended on him.

A large part of the finds of the Roman period are exhibited today in the **Roman-Germanic Museum**, built between 1970 and 1974 near the Cathedral, on the very spot where the *Dionysus Mosaic*, which can be dated back to about 220, was found in 1949, so that it could be displayed to the public in its place of origin.

From the spacious western window even a passing visitor can get an idea

There are numerous refined cult objects or items of everyday use that can be admired in the Roman-Germanic Museum.

Among them, numerous oil lamps, often with the representation of scenes of daily life or historical or even legendary characters.

Splendid glass objects, giving an idea of the high level of workmanship achieved.

Below, an original relief of the 3rd century in which a dog and a wild boar are represented, with reference to a quotation from a disciple of Diogenes.

of the rich culture of the first centuries after the birth of Christ. The *Sepulcher of Poblicius,* 14.6 metres high, towers over everything. The museum gives an idea of what life was like in ancient times, giving examples of various kinds, from daily life to religious functions, from journeys to trade and work, and from simple living to the luxuries of the rich. Of particular interest are the glass laboratory and ceramics products of Cologne, which were found near the Roman tower on the Gereonstrasse and at Eigelstein. Fine white sand, which came from the Frechen area, was an indispensable raw material in obtaining high-quality products. The compound, prepared according to complicated recipes, was made to dissolve in a fireproof oven and then worked once again at a temperature that reached 1200 degrees. This produced the glass objects whose rich colours and elegant shapes we can admire today.

More views and works from the extraordinary Roman-Germanic Museum of Cologne, which provides a fascinating and detailed picture of the city and its many splendours during the Roman age.

Note particularly, on the right, a splendid example of a cameo, again from the Roman age.

The spectacular reconstruction of a large room which in classical times it was normal to find in luxurious Roman villas. The vast original mosaic gives an idea of what the floor of the sumptuous Roman residence, discovered next to the Cathedral of Cologne, must have been like. On the walls, again with the help of original finds, a realistic reconstruction of the decoration has been made, against a rich red background of Pompeian derivation.

Eau de Cologne

The most celebrated of all scented waters takes its name from the city of Cologne. If its origins and composition are shrouded in legend, its fame in modern times is instead unequivocal. From the 17th century this splendid perfume was exported throughout the world, became immensely popular in Europe and was loved and used by such important figures and celebrities as Napoleon, Goethe, Voltaire and Queen Victoria.

The secret of the success of eau de cologne is the highly refreshing mixture of different perfumes: *oils of neroli*, *bergamot*, *lavender* and *rosemary* and numerous other essences amounting to a total of thirty different ingredients. Its origins, however, are not those of a simple perfume: "*aqua mirabilis*" was once the term used for this mixture of etheric oils and diluted ethanol, considered a universal remedy useful in treating any ailment, from a sore throat to gout and plague. Only later did it come to be used as a toiletry product. French troops used to call the scented water "*Eau de Cologne*", a name used until 1914, when the German version "*Kölnisch Wasser*" was officialized. Today the denomination "*Echt Kölnisch Wasser*" is a protected geographical indication.

The attribution of the formula of *Eau de Cologne* to its actual inventor is highly controversial. There were many master perfume-makers who attempted to counterfeit the formula and attribute to themselves the merit of having produced the new fragrance, so refreshing and smooth compared to the heavy perfumes typical of the age. There were numerous trials against counterfeiting companies: in 1865, in Cologne alone, there were as many as thirty-nine!

Some sources attest that the real inventor was the Italian Giovanni Paolo Feminis, who upon his death passed on the formula to his assistant Giovanni Maria Farina, an Italian merchant who had immigrated to Germany. In 1806 his grandson would found in Paris the Jean-Marie Farina, which was later sold to Roger et Gallet. Giovanni Maria Farina described his *aqua mirabilis* as follows: like "an Italian spring morning after the rain. It reminds me of oranges, lemons, grapefruits, bergamots, citrons, the flowers and aromatic herbs of my homeland. It refreshes and stimulates my senses and imagination".

Glockengasse 4711

On Glockengasse, at number 4711, is the historical site of the celebrated Eau de Cologne 4711. Here for over two centuries has stood the house of Wilhelm Mülhens, who received the recipe for the precious *aqua mirabilis* from a Charterhouse monk on the day of his marriage. In 1796 the French troops occupied Cologne and reorganized the numbering of the streets, giving to the house and the workshop the number 4711. From 1875 this became the registered trade-mark of the "Real Eau de Cologne". On the south facade of the building is a musical box which every hour moves to the sound of the Marseillaise. Inside, a large tapestry made in 1864 illustrates the scene in which a French soldier attributed to the house the number that would later become famous.

The Farina Perfume Museum

At Obenmarspforten 21, the historical headquarters of the Farina family, is the Farina Perfume Museum, adorned with the celebrated fire-red tulip, the family symbol. In the laboratory of the master perfumer, accompanied by the music of Carlo Farina, visitors can follow the stages in the making of the perfume, from the choice of the essence to the *enfleurage*, up to the preservation of the precious product. Exhibited inside are the flasks designed to contain the scents: from small elongated bottles sealed with wax, to sturdier and therefore more easily transportable "champagne" bottles.

On these pages, images associated with the celebrated eau de Cologne; the street number of its historic production centre has become an unmistakable trademark, famous all over the world.

The Cathedral

Above, the "Nadelöhr", the side arch of the northern Roman gate, near the Cathedral.

Right, a striking image of the apse of the Cathedral; below, a view of the elaborate buttresses bristling with spires and pinnacles.

The Cathedral, with its high towers, the symbol and centre of Cologne, bears witness to over 1900 years of the city's history. From the year 50, in the northeast corner of the Roman town, a temple rose dedicated to Mercury Augustus, similar to the one in Rome consecrated to the Goddess Fortuna. Between the cathedral and the walls lay a piece of ground owned by the Church. In 313, when the Church obtained its freedom at the time of the first bishop, Maternus, the existence of an ecclesiastical building over 130 metres long was certified on this ground. Access is gained to the baptistery from the east, on the side of the Rhine. One then passes along a habitable wing, reaching the atrium at the top of a flight of stairs, which contains

HOTEL

on three sides the Roman temple, followed by the episcopal church which is almost 40 metres long.

In around 565, when the early church was no longer sufficient, Bishop Carentius enlarged the atrium, thus creating the second Cathedral, a building almost 85 metres long, which was further enlarged and completed by Bishop Hildebold, friend and advisor to Charlemagne, on the model of the Monastery of St. Gallener.

When Hildebold became archbishop and metropolitan of the new province, which by that stage extended from Belgium to Hamburg, he completed the project of a new, even larger Cathedral, which was begun in 818 and consecrated in 870. Thanks to finds now available to us, we have reliable information on the various buildings which existed before the Cathedral from the Roman age onwards.

Precious manuscripts from the Hildebold period are presently kept in the Cathedral library, while others are on display in the treasury. After his return from a journey to Rome, Archbishop Bruno, brother of Emperor Otto I, brought some reliquaries, but the most outstanding works among those that were transferred from the Roman Cathedral to the Gothic one are the *Cross of Gero,* which he had sculpted after his journey to Byzantium (before 976) and the *Reliquary of the Three Kings.*

After his conquest of Milan, Emperor Frederick Barbarossa sent his chancellor in Italy, the archbishop of Cologne Rainald of Dassel, the bones of the Three Kings as precious spoils of war. In 1164 they were moved to Hildebold's Cathedral, amidst cries of joy from the crowd. Cologne thus became one of the most important destinations for pilgrims in the world. In 1181, one of the leading goldsmiths of the time, Nicholas of Verdun, started working on the *Reliquary of the Three Kings*, which, once finished in 1230, was a work of value unequalled throughout the world. Later, in 1248, the Cathedral Chapter decided to build the Gothic Cathedral, which according to plans at

Above, the statue of the Virgin Mary with Child, the sacred intermediary between the Old and New Testament, who seems to be welcoming the faithful from the top of the main door of the Cathedral.

Right, an elegant and highly original decorative element from the doors of the Cathedral.

Left, the main facade of Cologne Cathedral; below, a detail of its central door; above, the south door, at the south end of the transept.

the time was to be larger and in the centre of which the bones were to be placed. In 1288 the town councillors engraved the three crowns in the city's coat-of-arms, where they still are today. In 1961-1973, the *Reliquary* was restored to its former splendour by the goldsmiths Fritz Zegruber and Peter Bolg, after deterioration suffered over eight hundred years of history.

The figured part of the *Reliquary of the Three Kings* is a real theological *summa*. The side panels of the lower strip symbolize in the portrayal of the Prophets surrounding King David and Solomon the revelation of God to the Jewish people. The front part, worked in pure gold, consists of the central figure of Christ, seated in the Virgin Mary's lap, and of the adoration of the Magi bearing gifts. They represent the pagan world which, guided by the star, finds its way to Jesus. God has always shown himself to man not only through words, but also through natural phenomena. In the upper part of the reliquary is Christ Pantocrator surrounded by the twelve apostles who will judge and save the nations with their words and teachings when the end of the world occurs. The rear part portrays the Passion and Transfiguration of Christ.

One of the most noteworthy displays inside Cologne Cathedral is the *Cross of Gero* which commemorates the visit of the archbishop to Byzantium in 971 on behalf of Otto I to ask Princess Theophanu's hand in marriage. It is the oldest and largest crucifix in the Western world and was previously the pride of Hildebold's Romanesque cathedral.

Above, the monumental wooden crucifix donated by Archbishop Gero in about 970.

Left, the stunning and extremely precious *Reliquary of the Three Kings* (1180-1230).

Right, the vast space of the nave of Cologne Cathedral, one of the highest in the world.

On this page, two images of the so-called "Pentecost window", made in the middle of the 19th century.
The central scene represents the descent of the Holy Spirit on the day of the Pentecost (here on the left), traditionally considered to be the birth day of the Church. This explains the presence of the scene at the top of the stained-glass window, in which Peter is represented as he receives the keys of the Kingdom of Heaven (below).

The Cathedral's wooden chancel, with its 104 stalls, was completed in about 1330 and is richly inlaid with scenes depicting episodes of daily life, which are a true reflection of human states of mind. During his visit on 15 November 1980, Pope John Paul II sat down in one of these stalls as a reminder that at one time both the Pope and the Emperor were canons of Cologne Cathedral.

Even today the multi-coloured *stained-glass windows* give the cathedral's interior a unique appearance. The windows of the nave and side chapels are considered models of glass-painting in Germany on account of their width, brilliance and perfection. They are set against the five large windows in flamboyant Gothic style of the north aisle, considered one of the masterpieces of medieval glass-painting.

In the 19th century, the cathedral was enriched with important works of art from secularized churches. Some of the destroyed cathedral windows were rebuilt by utilizing the stained-glass windows of these churches, salvaged thanks to the intervention of the canon, Ferdinand Wallraf. In his book *The Medieval Stained-Glass Window of Cologne Cathedral*, Herbert Rode asserts that the stained-glass windows, comprising over 4100 pieces, with figures, buildings and ornamentation, stylistically reflects the evolution of glass-painting in Cologne during the period from 1260 to 1562.

The *Bible Windows* deserve a special mention. The oldest one, which felt the influence of the Romanesque style, was created before 1260. Divided into two parts, it illustrates in ten panels the New and Old Testaments, beginning with the creation of Eve up to the Ascension of Christ. The images with the Virgin Mary, who gave the world its Saviour and with Christ Almighty stand out from the others in that they bear a decoration symbolizing

the signs of royalty. The second bible window, in a similar way to the previous one, was donated before 1280 by Albertus Magnus and by Archbishop Siegfried von Westerburg to the Dominican church which once rose where the General Post Office now stands. It was Wallraf who salvaged the window after the demolition of the church in 1804, transferring it to the Cathedral in 1823. Today it is placed in the Chapel of St. Stephen, behind the altar of the Patrons of the City by Stephan Lochner.

What strikes one most on entering the Cathedral is its extraordinary height. The external length of the building is 144.58 metres and the tower is 157.38 metres high; the nave is 119 metres long and 43.35 metres high. The windows of the nave, with 48 images of kings, are 17 metres high, while those of the aisles are 19.8 metres high. A gallery with three-light windows runs the entire length of the church, joining together and harmonizing the various architectural elements. The stained-glass windows, which cover a total surface of 10,000 m^2 – 1,500 of which depict episodes from the Gospel – give light and lightness to the building.

The lower part of the apse features the 5-metre high *Group of Apostles,* whose canopies are crowned by angels playing music.

Together with the *Stained-Glass Window of the Bible*, other masterpieces of previous centuries were kept inside the Cathedral after the French Revolution, where they still are today and where they will remain. The most important of these are the altar of the Poor Clares near the Roman tower and the altar of the patrons of the city, the work of Stephan Lochner, which comes from the City Hall Chapel.

The *Klarenaltar* is on three different levels, illustrating the various phases of the Salvation. In the level

Donated by King Ludwig I in 1847 and installed on the south side of the Cathedral the following year, at the time of the celebrations for the sixth centenary of the beginning of work on the building of the Cathedral, this large stained-glass window is dedicated to the Lamentation over the Dead Christ, with a representation of the Last Supper in the upper part.

used on religious holidays, the twelve Apostles are portrayed and the bottom features the twelve virgins; the second level, used during public holidays and on Sundays, describes the Annunciation and the life of Jesus up to the Passion and his ascent to heaven, whereas the third level depicts saints who led an exemplary life with a spirit of Franciscan devotion. The altar, which dates back to 1350-1400, was brought back to the Cathedral once again after a restoration that lasted almost thirty years.
The *Altar of the Wise Men,* the "Patrons of the City", created by Stephan Lochner in 1442-1445, today is simply called the "Image of the Cathedral". In its centre the three richly clothed Wise Men, surrounded by their retinue, offer gifts to Christ who is in the Virgin Mary's lap; at the sides, St. Gereon and St. Ursula, together with their gaily-coloured retinue, pay homage to Christ. The Angels' Annunciation to the Virgin Mary is depicted in the background. Together with other important works in the Cathedral, it is evidence of the artistic production of a religious nature dating back to that century in the Rhine-Dutch area.

The thirteenth (above) and the fourteenth are instead free-standing sculptural groups with dimensions that exceed natural size. All were made at the end of the 19th century by Wilhelm Mengelberg.

The Via Crucis of Cologne Cathedral is punctuated by the usual fourteen stations of the Cross, identified by devotional images. Of these, twelve have been executed in high relief and painted (above and right).

We arrived at the name of the author of this work of art through Albrecht Dürer, who described a visit to Cologne in his diary, during which he had the curator show him the painting at least twice. At that time it was still kept in the Chapel of the City Hall, for which it was originally commissioned. Only after the destruction of the chapel was the work of art transferred to the Cathedral. Stephan Lochner (1400-1451) left us his self-portrait in the central figure of St. Gero's door panel. The thin hand of the artist contrasts with the grip of the double sword; the left hand grasps the arm of a pupil, deeply moved at the sight of the gifts of the Wise Men.

The present Gothic Cathedral, begun on 15 August 1248 by Archbishop Konrad von Hochstaden (1238-1261), is the fifth building erected on that site. On 27 September 1322, Archbishop Heinrich von Virneburg, during a provincial meeting, solemnly consecrated the east chancel, of which certain parts have remained including the altar and choir-stalls. A wall with a stained-glass window separated the Gothic chancel from the part of the old Cathedral that still existed, where works were to continue until 1560. Some of the enlargements were done by members of the Parler family, relatives of Peter Parler, to whom we owe the Cathedral of Prague.

In 1395 the first floor of the south tower was completed. The figures on the portal were replaced by copies, while the originals for the time being are in safekeeping in the Diocesan Museum (Kolumba). The part between the south tower and the dividing wall was used as from 1388 as the chapel of the University which was opened in that period. In 1507-1508 the five magnificent stained-glass windows in the north wall were installed. It was only in 1842 that Archbishop Cardinal von Geissel and the King of Prussia Frederick William IV laid the foundation stone of the extension of the Cathedral, which was enthused over by Georg Forster (1790), Friedrich von Schlegel (1804), Joseph Görres (1814) and many others and on which Sulpiz Boisserée worked tirelessly. On 15 October 1880, in the presence of Emperor William I, the last stone of the south tower was laid: the Cathedral was finally finished after 632 years of work.

But it was necessary to start working on it again for the third time. In 1904 the Cathedral was badly damaged by atmospheric agents. The Supervisor of Works, Hertel (1903-1927), opened a new construction site in order to restore it. During the Second World War the Cathedral was hit by 14 bombs. Ten vaults of the upper nave and

Above, the triptych known as "Image of the Cathedral", painted around 1442 by Stephan Lochner, the most important expression of the late Gothic school of painting in Cologne. The wings of the altarpiece are closed during Advent and Lent.

Below, the *Klarenaltar*, the "Altar of the Poor Clares", a highly original work with its three different levels.

The belfry of Cologne Cathedral houses twelve bells, each with its own particular sound.

Below, the so-called "Bell of St Peter".

four vaults of the side aisle collapsed. All that remained for the new Supervisor of Works, Weyres (1944-1972), was to make the chancel utilizable by 15 August 1948, the seven hundredth anniversary of its foundation. In 1956 the west part was once again ready to celebrate mass. But work still goes on, under the direction of A. Wolff, who together with 60 workers is engaged in a struggle to combat damage caused by atmospheric agents and pollution. And that struggle continues to this day, now that the Cathedral of Cologne has been included in UNESCO's list of world heritage sites (1996). The inhabitants of Cologne have resigned themselves. A popular saying goes: "When work on the Cathedral is finished, the world will come to an end".

Right, another unusual detail of Cologne Cathedral.

Below, the Hohenzollern Bridge that seems to stretch out towards the Cathedral and the Old City crossing the Rhine.

Cologne during the Pastoral Period: The 12 Romanesque Churches

One of the most prosperous periods in Cologne's history were the three centuries under the archbishops' rule, starting with Bruno, the younger brother of Emperor Otto I. In 881 the Normans sacked and set fire to the city, which had already lost importance during the tumults, migrations and strife among the families of the Franks. But not only Norman ships arrived in Cologne; the rapid cavalry of the Danube arrived from Hungary, erupting several times in the town, until Otto I reached a truce by paying a tribute; this gave him a chance to train a powerful army on horseback, which in 955 defeated the Hungarians in the Battle of Lechfeld, thus enabling a period of peaceful reconstruction. To put an end to controversies between ducal families, Emperor Otto I supported the bishops and their temporal power. And that is how his faithful younger brother Bruno (953-965) became the grand duke of Lorraine and archbishop of Cologne. In twelve years of enlightened government, he brought the city back to new splendour. He included the Rhine island in the Roman walls, extending the walled area from 100 to 125 hectares, therefore providing greater security, especially to tradesmen. Spiritually he belonged to the group of the St. Benedictine order which depended on the Abbey of Gorze, which he then called St. Pantaleon, and which later became a stronghold of art and science. His tomb is to be found in this abbey today. The important monasteries of St. Andreas, St. Aposteln, Great St. Martin and St. Maria im Kapital are still linked to his name.

The peak of the period of development that started with him was reached in 1200. And in fact the Romanesque churches that still today constitute the wealth and pride of Cologne because of their exceptional character date back to that period. They were badly damaged during the last war. Large contributions for their reconstruction have been given not only by the Church, the city and the whole country, but also by the "Association in support of the reconstruction of Romanesque churches", supported by members of all sects, who have reattracted the public's attention above all to the twelve churches of that period: St. Andreas, St. Aposteln, St. Cecilia's, St. Georg, St. Gereon, Great St. Martin, St. Kunibert, St. Maria im Ka-

A delightful little area of Cologne; in the background the impressive and unmistakable tower of Great St. Martin church.

pitol, St. Maria Lyskirchen, St. Pantaleon, St. Severin and St. Ursula. These twelve churches remind us of the nineteen impressive churches and monasteries that around 1200 characterized the life and appearance of the city.
The 13th century witnessed the splendour and power of the Hohenstaufens, but also their decline. With Frederick II (1212-1250) concentrating his objectives in Italy, Sicily and the Mediterranean, imperial power declined in Germany. Those who held spiritual and temporal power were deprived of their privileges; self-government and military supremacy were reached. In Cologne the townsmen defeated the archbishop at the battle near Worringen in 1288; from then onwards he was able to enter the city only with the Council's permission. His right as bishop and elector to elect the King, granted to him

Images from the Church of St Andreas: the the left, the *Maccabees Shrine*, created between 1520 and 1527 by Peter Hanemann to house the relics of the Maccabees, the Jewish brothers who were martyred in the 2nd century BC; below left, the altar panel of the Confraternity of the Rosary, known also as the "Madonna with the cloak", the work of the Master of St. Severin datable to around 1510; below, one of the old wall paintings.

by the golden seal in 1356, was in violated during the course of the civil strife in the city.
When the inhabitants of Cologne appointed their beloved Cardinal Fring freeman on 22 June 1967, they caused the re-emergence of this dispute, which had been forgotten for a long time.
The **church of St. Andreas**, built by Archbishop Bruno (953-965) rises up almost in front of the Cathedral towers. In the present building, the late Romanesque (about 1200) and late Gothic (about 1420) naves form a harmonious unit, characterized by an evident elevation. The crypt, which was filled with earth at the beginning of the 15th century, was opened up again in 1953 and today contains the sarcophagus of Albertus Magnus.
One can admire the *painting of the Rosary,* attributed to the Maestro of St. Severin in 1510, which hangs to the right of the side chapel, under ornaments and vestments of various centuries. This painting recalls the foundation in 1474 of the Honorable Confraternity of the Rosary, which counted the Emperor Frederick III among its members and was present in Cologne in 1475 during the declaration of Cologne as a free city of the Empire.
The **church of St. Aposteln** at Neumarkt is a masterpiece of Romanesque architecture in the Rhineland, crowning the city. It was built during the 9th century, whereas the three-foiled chancel was added in 1192.
St. Heribert, situated on the opposite bank of the Rhine at Cologne-Deutz, is not one of the twelve Romanesque churches mentioned above. It is, however, proof of the deep friendship that bound the archbishop of Cologne to Emperor Otto III during the years 990-1021; in fact, the emperor promised the archbishop on his deathbed that he would found a monastery, the present St. Heribert. The saint's *reliquary* has survived to this day: this work, dating back to about 1170, is an example of the artistic wealth of goldsmiths in Cologne at the time of Frederick Barbarossa, a member of the Hohenstaufen family. The reliquary, 153 cm long, 42 cm wide and

Above, an old picture representing the church of St. Cecilia next to the larger church dedicated to St. Peter.

Below, another of the splendid works of art that can be admired in the church of St. Aposteln: an expressive Saint Michael the Archangel.

Church of St. Aposteln: above, the splendid neo-Gothic altarpiece of 1910 which contains a 16th-century sculpture of the Madonna and Child.

In the old St. Cecilia, with the support of new adjoining buildings and fascinating displays, is housed, in the Schnütgen Museum, one of the most important collections of medieval art in Europe. Next to it, in what survives of the old church and monastery of St. Peter, is the seat of an important art centre, the Kunst Station St. Peter.

Below, one of the precious frescoed ceilings (13th century) of St. Maria Lyskirchen, the smallest of the twelve Romanesque churches in Cologne.

68 cm high, is in silver and copper sheet that is gilded, enamelled and enriched by filigree and stones: the front part portrays the mother of God, seated on a throne flanked by two angels, while the back part depicts St. Heribert, flanked by allegorical figures of Humility and Charity. On the sides, are enamel representations of the Apostles, surrounded by prophets and holding open two books in which the verses of the Creed are inscribed. The upper and lower surfaces are divided into six parts: each of the large enamel medallions relates a scene from the life of a saint.

The **church of St. Cecilia's** recalls an important girls' college where the archbishop traditionally celebrated the second Christmas Mass. The precious collection of the **Schnütgen Museum** is kept in the present church, which dates back to 1150-1170. It is the only old collegiate church which, together with a parish church (St Peter), survived

Precious works of art in St. Maria im Kapitol: above, the so-called "Madonna of Limburg" (13th century); below, a detail of the carved door jambs; right, the original screen between the nave and apse on which the modern pipe organ stands.

the secularization of 1803. It was used as a chapel for the Civilian Hospital, destroyed during the Second World War.

At the end of the 7th century, where the Roman capitoline temple originally stood, **St. Maria im Kapitol** was built by Plectrude, the wife of Pepin of Herstal. Archbishop Anno consecrated the building in 1065. After restoration work, made necessary by the damage it suffered during the last war, Cardinal Hoffner was able once again to celebrate Holy Mass at Christmas 1984, thus continuing the old tradition according to which the archbishop of Cologne celebrates Midnight Mass every Christmas. Worthy of interest are the doors, dating from 1050, which illustrate the life of Christ in 26 high reliefs, starting with the Annunciation and ending with the descent of the Holy Spirit. In this wooden door we find the style used in ivory reliefs of this period.

St. Georg, which was built over Roman walls, is the only pre-Romanesque basilica with columns to have survived in the Rhineland. It was founded by Archbishop Anno in 1059. The massive building to the west is also one of its kind; from the outside, it looks like an

inarticulate cubic block, yet inside, with the three tympanums of the arches and its division on two floors, it has an unexpected lightness. The building dates from 1188.

St. Maria Lyskirchen, dating from the 10th century, is situated outside the old walls in the port district and today it still looks over the Rhine port. The present building in the Romanesque style was built in about 1220. Despite modifications made in later centuries, the old ceiling frescoes remained as they were until 1934, when they were restored to their original splendour. In 1947, damage from the last war, fortunately not too serious, was repaired. On the ceilings and walls, one can admire one of the largest series of frescoes by Rhineland artists of the 13th century.

St. Severin, together with the Cathedral, St. Gereon and St. Ursula, is one of the oldest churches in Cologne. Its history began in the 4th century. The eastern part of the crypt and the Romanesque chancel were completed before 1237. Evidence of the original furnishing of the church is constituted by the enamelled image of the saint, at present in the Diocesan Museum (Kolumba); this image was found in the saint's reliquary of the 11th century, unfortunately destroyed during the French Revolution. St. Severin is closely associated with the great 15th-century masters of panel painting, such as the Master of St. Veronica or the Master of St. Severin, some of whose works are still in the church. The **fortifications** are also evidence of Cologne's glorious past. Archbishop Bruno had enlarged the Roman city, creating the residential area of the traders, situated towards the bank of the Rhine. In 1106 the townsfolk, encouraged by their military sovereignty, increased the area of the city, which went from 125 to 217 hectares. The third expansion was made from 1180, with the incorporation of St. Severin, St. Pantaleon, St. Mauritius and St Gereon. The area of the city was protected by 12 gates and by 52 towers incorporated into the walls, of which are still preserved the Gate of Severin, the Hahnentor and the Eigelsteintorburg.

St. Pantaleon is one of the few churches from the period of the Ottonian dynasty, that is, dating from the second half of the 10th century. The impressive building is the expression of imperial grandeur and the high level reached by German and foreign art. It takes us back to the time of the Saxon emperors and reminds us of the Empress Theophanes, who wished to be buried here like

Above, the tower of the church of St. Severin.

Left, the Severin Gate, one of the 12 gates incorporated into the city walls following the third phase of the city's expansion.

Right, the west side of the very old church of St. Pantaleon, dating from the period of the Ottonian dynasty.

Archbishop Bruno. During the Romanesque period there was an important goldwork and miniatures laboratory near St. Pantaleon.

St. Gereon is the largest church of the Romanesque period. It was built on the remains of a decagonal plan construction dating back to Roman times and richly decorated with magnificent mosaics; it was dedicated to the so-called "martyrs of the legion of Thebes", under the command of St. Gereon, who in about 300 was martyred together with the other legionaries, subsequently becoming patron of the city. According to Gregory of Tours, the bodies of the martyrs were thrown into a well which has not yet been found. It was not until 612 that the name "Basilica St. Gereonis Martyris" officially appeared. The Merovingians chose it as a church for coronations and commemorative services; it is the burial place for the bishops Hildebert, who died in 762, and Hildebold, who passed away in 818. As far back as 840 mention was made of the house for canons which existed until 1802. Well-known artists participated in its restoration after the Second World War, but it was only in 1984 that the church was again used for religious services.

The stained-glass windows, the work of Georg Meistermann and Wilhelm Buschulte, and the mosaics of the 11th-century floor, laid in the crypt on the wishes of Archbishop Anno to the central part of the choir-stalls,

Above, the eastern apse of St. Gereon (12th century); below, the decagonal cupola (1219-1227) with the great organ and an image of the splendid interior of the apse.

highlight, together with numerous ancient and modern works, the importance of this 48-metre high church, to the extent that it has been compared to Hagia Sophia in Istanbul or to Florence Cathedral. The present appearance of this church, which is the most important church in Cologne after the Cathedral, dates from the years 1219-1227.
St. Ursula and her virgins, together with St. Gereon and the Wise Men, are patrons of the city. Legend has it that Ursula suffered martyrdom at the hands of the Huns, who at the time were besieging Cologne, on her return from a pilgrimage to Rome together with her companions. The worship of the saint spread throughout Western Christendom. According to what has been confirmed by excavations, the **church of St. Ursula** dates back to about 400. The present Romanesque women's gallery was built in the 12th century and is the first example of its kind in the Lower Rhine. The eleven flames on the city's coat-of-arms symbolize St. Ursula and the virgins.
The oldest seal to have survived dates back to 1149; it is the seal of the city of Cologne with the inscription "Saint Cologne, through the grace of God faithful daughter of the Church of Rome". On this basis, the inhabitants of Cologne had their rights approved: in 1106 the right of fortification and military sovereignty, which led to the second extension of the city and, from 1180, the third extension, making Cologne the largest, most highly populated city in Germany. Findings of this grandeur are the doors, the remains of the walls and the house of the powerful Overstolzen family on the Rheingasse.
St. Kunibert, the last of the great Romanesque churches in Cologne, was consecrated in 1247, one year before the laying of the foundation stone of the Cathedral. Gothic elements prevail over the building's massive structure, giving it a solemn character and plenty of light. The church, which dates from the 7th century, was originally called St. Clements, a name that remained until 663, when Bishop Kunibert was buried. In 687, the two Anglo-Saxon missionaries named Ewald were buried here, whose reliquary was restored in the 19th century. In 1215, under the east chancel towards the Rhine, a crypt and a font were built which were particularly important for popular tradition, according to which the babies of Cologne come from "Kunibert's Font". The church furnishings include many precious objects, like the linen cloths of the reliquary dedicated to the two missionaries Ewald, of the 9th century, and the reliquary of 1220 which is in the church's Treasury. The stained-glass windows in the chancel and transept, dating from 1230, are among the most outstanding works of Romanesque stained-glass painting in Germany.
The **church of Great St. Martin** is a symbol of Cologne thanks to its impressive tower. Destroyed during the war, it had to be almost entirely rebuilt. The complex and radical restoration of its interior could be considered finished only in 1985. The trefoil chancel, which looks over the Rhine, is one of the most celebrated works of Romanesque

On this page, images of St. Ursula, where, in addition to other precious relics, the celebrated reliquary busts of the saint are conserved in the choir.

architecture. When the waters of the Rhine are high, it reminds us that the church really stands on an island which, at the time of Archbishop Bruno, was connected to the bank and enclosed within the city walls. It now stands in the centre of the old town which during the period immediately after the war was transformed into a recreational area for the inhabitants of the city and tourists. This church also reflects the high standard of local architecture reached during that important period that goes from 1150 to 1250.
The city of Cologne's then superintendent of monuments, Hiltrud Kier, wrote in the introduction to her large illustrated volume on the city's Romanesque churches (Cologne, 1985): "Cologne is the only city in the world with twelve large Romanesque churches still standing in its centre. During the Middle Ages it was the most important city in Germany and the third largest city in the world after Rome and Constantinople. The rich merchants of Cologne promoted the architectural embellishment of their city, whose surrounding walls, towered houses used for trading purposes, town hall and, in particular, churches provided an incomparable view for onlookers from the Rhine. All visiting merchants must have been impressed by this unforgettable sight, symbol of Cologne's wealth. The city's large number of saints, whose mortal remains were venerated in the Romanesque churches, attracting hordes of pilgrims, was enhanced in 1164 with the acquisition of the mortal remains of the Wise Men for the cathedral, which must be considered the monumental centre of the city's crown of churches".

Left page, the splendid interior of St. Kunibert.

On this page, the apse and unmistakable tower of the majestic church of Great St. Martin, whose imposing bulk towers behind typical little houses with pretty facades on the banks of the Rhine. Archeological excavations carried out in the 1960s, when the church still had to be restored after the wartime destruction, brought to light interesting remains of a previous ancient building datable to the 1st century (left).

Heinzelmännchenbrunnen
The Fountain of the Heinzelmännchen

A short distance from the Cathedral is an interesting little fountain associated with an ancient legend linked to the city. When Cologne was but a tiny village, the nights were animated by industrious *Heinzelmännchen*, house gnomes who devoted themselves to all the town chores: washing and cleaning, making bread, household tasks. When their work was done, they vanished. At that time the inhabitants of Cologne lazed around all day because when they woke in the morning they found all their activities mysteriously finished. This idyll came to an end one evening, when the wife of a tailor, unable to contain her curiosity, wanted at all costs to discover who brought the work to completion. During the night she scattered a handful of dried peas on the stairs, in such a way as to make any unknown visitor slip and fall. The little folk, caught *in flagrante*, were so indignant that they vanished and never came back to the town. From that day the lazy inhabitants of Cologne had to do all their chores themselves. This legend, transcribed by a teacher in 1826, inspired the painter and poet August Kopisch, who in 1836 made a poem from it (translated into English as 'The Little Fairies of Cologne').

The pretty and highly celebrated "Fountain of the Gnomes", almost a symbol of Cologne, and certainly the loveliest image of one of its most popular legends.

The Little Fairies of Cologne

How it once was
With fairies so nice!
Then, when man was lazy, he could lie
On a bench and look only after himself:
Then they came by night
As expected.
The little men would swarm
And turn and buzz
And pull
And pluck
And hop and trot
And clean and scrape...
And when a lazy bones awoke,
All his day's work was... already
finished.

The carpenters laid themselves
On the bench and stretched.
And then came the ghostly crowd
And saw, what there was to be
carpentered.
Take chisel and axe
And the saw in haste!
They sawed and stuck
And chopped and broke,
Coughed up
And cut back,
And took aim like hawks
And set the beams...
And when the carpenters saw...
Snap! stood the whole house ...
finished there!

With the bakers there was no
emergency,
The fairies baked bread.
The lazy lads lay around,
The fairies stirred themselves –
And groaning there
With sacks so heavy!
They kneaded heartily,
And labored furiously,
And beat
And shoved,
And scoured and baked
And pounded and chopped.
The lazy lads snored like a choir...
And shortly the bread was baked!

By the butcher it went the same:
Journeymen and apprentices lay in
peace.
At then came the little men there
And butchered the pig every which way.
It all went so fast
Like the mill wheel in the wind!
They banged with cleavers,
They sliced on the butcher's block,
They rinsed,
They rummaged,
And mingled and mixed
And filled and wiped.
When the journeymen opened their eyes...
Bang! the sausage hung ready for sale!

By school kids it was this way:
it holds
That they didn't stay home anymore.
Their homework just left undone,
But the fairies did that especially well.
They wrote quickly
Like the wind.
They added and painted,
They numbered and figured
And doodled
And clambered about,
They read, erased,
They made things, and copied.
And as the school kids expected...
QED! everything was accomplished.

Once a tailor had a great problem:
To finish a regal coat;
He dropped his tools and laid down
Since he didn't want to think about it.
Then they slipped in
Around the tailor's table:
They cut and adjusted
And sewed and stitched,
And fastened
And fit,
And stretched and looked
And pulled and jerked.
And when the tailor awoke...
The Mayor's coat was all made!

Curious was the tailor's wife
And she made it her own business:
She strew dried peas the other night
That the fairies might come to seek
them out:
One ventured out,
And was beaten in the house,
And one came down the stairs
And was caught by the tub,
They fell from
Buckles
They cried aloud and shouted
And screamed bloody murder!
She leapt after them hearing the
noise.
With the light: ssh, ssh, ssh, they were
all gone!

Alas! Now are they all disappeared
And none here any more!
One can't find the peace once had,
But must do everything himself!
One must be very diligent
In one's own work now,
And scratch and scrape
And run and trot
And spruce things up
And iron,
And pound and cut
And cook and bake
Alas, for it's not like it once was!
That lovely time
Will never come again!

Cologne up to the Thirty Years' War

As far back as the time of the archbishops' rule, Cologne had the right to unload goods transported on the Rhine. In 1259, Archbishop Konrad von Hochstaden guaranteed it to his "faithful" fellow-townsmen by their "request". Thanks to this right, Cologne became an important political and economic centre of world trade, especially with Holland and England, as could be seen at the international fairs held in spring and autumn which opened and closed to the ringing of the bells of Great St. Martin.

In 1367, Cologne reached the height of it commercial power. On 19 November of that year, in fact, representatives of the Hanseatic towns assembled in the City Hall of Cologne, put an end to the war against the Danish king Valdemar IV Atterdag, and obtained free trade in the Baltic Sea. In commemoration of this event the room in the City Hall where the agreement was signed is still named the "Hanseatic Hall", even though, if the truth be told, Cologne never took part in the battle. The 13th and 14th centuries were characterized not only by the aforementioned strife between townsmen and archbishops, but also by conflicts between the old families and the guilds which were acquiring more and more power. In 1396 there was open warfare, ending with the conquest of the statutes, which remained in force for 400 years up until the French Revolution. Evidence of this victory is the tower of the City Hall, 61 metres high, erected between 1407 and 1414 at the expense of the traders' families.

The Chapel, built in the southwest corner of the City Hall in 1426, became quite famous because in 1442-1445 Stephan Lochner painted for it the patrons of the city: *The Wise Men with St. Gereon and St. Ursula*. This painting, salvaged in 1800 by Franz Ferdinand Wallraf and given to the Cathedral in 1810, is known throughout the world as the "Image of the Cathedral".

Other famous religious works dating from the period between the 14th and the 16th centuries can be found in the churches of Cologne today. Among the masters of this age, we should mention Master Wilhelm, the earliest genealogist, author of the painting

Joos van Cleve, *Death of the Virgin*, first half of the 16th century, Wallraf-Richartz Museum.

of Veronica, and the Master of St. Severin, to whom we also owe the first painting of the Confraternity of the Rosary for the Dominican Church, at present in the church of St. Andreas. A series of even more important paintings of that period are to be found in the Wallraf-Richartz Museum, which bears the name of an art lover who saved many works of art before the French Revolution. Not even he, however, was able to prevent an even greater part of Cologne's religious artistic heritage from being destroyed after French occupation and secularization in 1803, or from being scattered throughout the world.

Of the buildings from that period, today we can still admire the **Gürzenich**, the festival hall built in 1437-1447, a series of typical middle-class houses and the **Storehouse on the Rhine** of 1558-1568. Almost all these monuments were bombed during the last war but have been restored to their former glory, giving us an idea of the power and splendour of Cologne.

1475 was a decisive year in the city's history. On 19 September, Emperor Frederick III, always favourably impressed by Cologne, bestowed on it the privilege of "free city of the Empire". This finally sealed its independence from the Prince Electors, which the townsmen of Cologne had conquered in 1288 at the battle of Worringen. It was the early Renaissance, when bourgeois families showed off their importance through their palaces. Even though the majority of them were bombed during the last war, some have been rebuilt and today we can admire their beauty. Individualism was the fundamental element of that period.

The portraits of Barthel Bruyn the Elder (1493-1556) show important tradesmen, mayors and scholars who represent the spirit and life of those decades. One must remember the art of printing, which from 1465 onwards played an important role in Cologne. Anton Woensam has handed down an image of the magnificence and beauty of Cologne during that period in his famous engraving of 1531, entitled *O Felix Agrippina Nobilis Romanorum Colonia* (Fortunate Agrippina, noble Roman colony). It represents the whole part of the city on the Rhine, from the Bayenturm to the fortifications near St. Kunibert. The Cathedral towers above the city; above the second floor of the south tower we can admire the crane which remained the symbol of Cologne until 1868, when the last phase of work on the Cathedral started.

German painter active in Cologne between 1410 and 1440, *Triptych*, datable between 1410 and 1440, Wallraf-Richartz Museum.

Too often history is passed down to us as a series of massacres, wars and catastrophies: events of this kind were certainly not lacking in Cologne's history. The massacre of Worringen in 1288, when the inhabitants of Cologne expelled the archbishop from the town, was preceded by civil strife, which did not ease even afterwards. The tower of the City Hall, for whose construction the families of the rich were condemned by the artisans, is enduring evidence of the struggles between the two social orders. Neither was there any shortage of calamities and epidemics, such as the plague that broke out in 1349 and which had far-reaching consequences. The year in which Stephan Lochner died, 1451, the plague was rife again. Persecutions and the expulsion of the Jews in 1424 give us an idea of the superstitious reaction that many had during that period. The Chapel of the City Hall, for which Stephan Lochner painted the Wise Men, today stands on the site of the old Synagogue, which had stood there for 300 years before being destroyed. The ritual bath, the "Mikvéh", was discovered due to the destructions of the war.

We also have records of the weavers' uprising in 1370. The sadness of the period is also revealed by works of art from that time, above all the *Crucifix of the Plague,* which was worshipped from 1304 at St. Maria im Kapitol. Men searched for and found comfort in religion: in the *Crucifix*, they saw the suffering of Christ and his Mother's grief portrayed and understood its spiritual meaning. On the contrary, the scenes painted by Stephan Lochner depict a more peaceful world, where angels play musical instruments and exult while they encircle the *Madonna of the Roses,* or they ascend to heaven in the painting of the *Last Judgement.* Albrecht Dürer, with his painting portraying a drummer and a flute-player propagandizing war, has given us an opposite example of that offered by the master of Cologne, which is instead an invitation to peace.

In the period of need, the orders of mendicant friars,

Above, Albrecht Dürer, *Piper and Drummer*, ca. 1504, Wallraf-Richartz Museum.
Below, Canaletto, *View of the Grand Canal*, ca. 1735, Wallraf-Richartz Museum.

especially the Franciscans and Dominicans, showed a good example with their vow of poverty, and through their sermons they helped many people. The **Minoritenkirche**, completed in 1260, which attracts numerous visitors because it contains the tombs of Duns Scotus (who died in 1308) and Adolf Kolping (who died in 1865), is also characteristic of that period due to its simplicity. Towards the end of the Gothic period, Cologne was a real artistic centre. About 350 paintings dating back to this period have survived. The size of this heritage is due to the fact that Cologne was spared the destruction perpetrated by the Reformation and to the collectionism of people like Hüpsch, Wallraf and the Boisserée brothers, who managed to rescue numerous works of art. In fact, a vast number of works of art were produced at the time. It is estimated that only 2-3% of the original production has survived.

Italian artist active in Lucca around 1260, *Enthroned Madonna and Child*, ca. 1260, Wallraf-Richartz Museum.

Below, Vincent van Gogh, *Le pont-levis* (*Drawbridge at Arles*), 1888, Wallraf-Richartz Museum.

Many of the works produced in these centuries are currently in the **Wallraf-Richartz Museum**, one of the most important art galleries in Germany, created in 1824 and then housed in a building erected on the site of an old monastery of minor friars (today replaced by a much more modern building). The church was rebuilt after being heavily damaged during the war and today it is the only Franciscan church in Cologne. In 1229 Franciscan friars founded their first monastery near St. Severin. In 1244 they moved the monastery to the old parish of Kolumba and started building the church, whose choir-stalls were consecrated in 1260. The soaring ribbed vaults revealed the new ideas of Gothic architecture. The walls are lightened by mullioned windows. The simplicity of the exterior and the sobriety of the interior of the building, without a transept and completely unadorned, express the ideal of poverty and the total devotion of the Franciscan friars. Restoration on the church after the Second World War, when a fire caused the vaults to collapse, was completed in 1958. None of the ancient interior decorations were saved. The stained-glass windows produced by Kaldenhoff in 1963 perfectly complement the

lack of colour in the interior. The magnificently coloured *Alsfeld Altarpiece,* dating from about 1480, invites visitors to prayer and meditation. People from all over the world come here to pray on the tomb of Adolf Kolping (beatified by John Paul II in 1991), who, at a time when Marx and Engels were inciting the class struggle, fought for corporative and social reform in young workers' associations. Evidence of Cologne's love for festivities is the **Gürzenich,** with its reception hall and ballroom built between 1437 and 1444. It is the most important town building in the Gothic style, where many guests were entertained, including emperors and prince electors. Since 1955 it has again been used for formal events, and following the radical restoration of 1997 it is also popular as a venue for conventions, balls and music concerts. The fact that it is so close to the ruins of the **church of St. Alban** seems to remind one how close life and death are. In the midst of the pillars and arches still standing in the church after the wartime destruction (only the facade on the street has been recently restored), the mourning figures of the parents of Käthe Kollwitz invite us to reflect on those killed in wars, both at home and abroad,

On these pages, suggestive images of the "Stadtmuseum Kölnisches", the City of Cologne History Museum, housed in the town's former 17th-century shipyard. It provides in-depth coverage of the political, economic and cultural history of Cologne from the Middle Ages to the present day.

and insistently appeal for peace. Another commemorative place, only a couple of hundred metres away and near the Opera House, is to be found among the ruins of the old **church of St. Kolumba**. Between 1457 and 1533, the Romanesque building was enlarged in the Gothic style. The statue portraying the Virgin Mary is still standing, despite bomb attacks during the war; this fact was considered a miracle by the inhabitants of Cologne, who called the statue *Madonna among the ruins.* In 1950 Gottfried Böhm, the son of the well-known church builder, Dominikus Böhm, constructed a small, central-plan building in a polygonal shape, which has become a popular place of worship among Cologne's inhabitants. Between 2003 and 2007 on this site, incorporating the remains of it with masterful skill, a building has been erected that today houses the **Kolumba**, a new museum of

religious art that is heir to the historic Diocesan Museum.
Of the town buildings in Cologne, the **City Hall** is number one from the historic and geographic points of view. Built on top of the Roman Town Hall, remains of which are to be found underground, it is in itself an embodiment of the city's history, starting from 1130 when it was called the Hanseatic Hall, on the walls of which are depicted the nine Good Heroes and the eight Prophets, dating from 1410. The Renaissance vestibule of 1569-1573, which is still standing, with the relief representing Samson, Daniel and Burgomaster Grin struggling with the lion (a funny episode in the city's history), causes one to reflect on the violent struggles that were rife in the city at the time.
The spiritual upheavals at the beginning of the modern age, around 1500, were also felt in Cologne, which nonetheless remained faithful to the old tradition; the city opened to Humanism but did not forget the ideals of the past. It is significant that the plan of the town made by Mercator in 1571 also included Roman elements in the margin. The atrium of the Town Hall (1567-1571), the

landing-stage on the Rhine (1558-1568) and the Shipyard (1596-1602) bear witness to the intense building activity of the middle classes in this period. The Reformation failed to take hold in Cologne: the reformist attempts of Archbishops Hermann von Wied (in 1547) and Gebhard Truchsess von Waldburg (in 1582) failed; the city remained faithful to the old religion and both were forced to resign. From 1584 the Papal Nuncios established themselves in Cologne; in 1583 Ernst von Bayer, the first of the five Wittlesbachs, became archbishop of Cologne. Nonetheless, there were very close ties with the Protestant Netherlands: Rubens lived for several years in Cologne, and the Church of St. Laurenz, near the City Hall, was once a Dutch college.

Below, the elegant historic City Hall of Cologne, fronted by the Renaissance style loggia.

Right, the majestic bronze wall built in 2007 by Ernst Wille next to the City Hall, around which there are numerous modern buildings.

The Renaissance and Baroque

It was Archbishop von Bayer who first established relations with the masters of the Renaissance and Baroque in southern Germany. Large residential buildings are to be found in Brühl and Bonn. In Cologne, on the other hand, alongside monasteries one finds only furnishings and altar ornaments and vestments, including a series of priest's habits, now in the Clementine Chapel of the Cathedral, which the Archbishop and Elector Clement August I had made in Lyon in 1742 especially for the crowning of his brother Charles VII as Emperor in Frankfurt. It is worth mentioning the gold monstrance of 1657, stolen from the Cathedral on the night between the 1 and 2 November 1975, during a storm; the work of Christian Schweling the Elder, the monstrance was a gift of the Archbishop Maximilian Heinrich. The most important work of this period is the *reliquary of Engelbert* for the Cathedral, which Konrad Duisberg completed in 1633; the figures portrayed are the work of Jeremias Geisselbrunn. Artists of that period came mainly from Holland or southern Germany, like the author of the project for the construction of the Maria Himmelfahrtskirche (1618-1627), Christoph Wamser, who was from Aschaffenburg. Other churches worth mentioning are that of St. Maria vom Frieden in der Schnurgasse (to whose Carmelite fathers the queen of France Maria de' Medici, exiled to Cologne, donated a miraculous image), the church of St. Maria in der Kupfergasse (1705-1715) and St. Ursula (1706-1712). The Elendskirche, built in the years 1765-1778 according to design by Balthasar Spaeth of the Groote family, should also be noted. This was also destroyed during the terrible night of 29 June 1943, but was later rebuilt.

On 6 October 1794, the first French revolutionary troops entered the city across the Hahnentor: the freedom of the "free city of the Empire" was coming to an end. The **church of St. Maria Himmelfahrt**, with its adjoining monastery of the Jesuits, who had arrived in Cologne in 1544, was declared a "Dekadentempel" and a prostitute was placed on the high altar as the goddess of Reason. The new propagators of revolutionary ideas thus began their battle against Christians, churches, priests and monasteries. Thanks however to their strenuous resistance, the townsfolk formally obtained freedom of wor-

The unmistakable houses of the Alter Markt seen behind the monument erected in 1884 to Jan von Werth, the mercenary soldier of the Thirty Years' War.

ship from Paris. The year 1796 marked the end of the worship of the goddess of Reason and St. Maria Himmelfahrtskirche was assigned to the Central School which rented it to the highest bidder, the tradesman Lorenz Fürth who, with the help of friends, obtained it for 300 thalers per year.

On the 9th November 1799, Napoleon ended the revolution with his coup d'état. He had understood that solid order in the church was a necessary condition for the establishment of a really new system; he thus declared the end of the Concordat between the Holy See and the French government. As a result, it was once again allowed to celebrate mass and Lorenz Fürth was once more able to make the church available for its original use. Some courageous men, like himself, saved many works of great cultural value from certain destruction; many others, however, took the opportunity to grow richer. In this way, about 150 churches and monasteries of Cologne, whose names are remembered by streets and squares, were destroyed.

The guarantee of freedom of worship did not stop all the Church property from being declared State property and, as from 1797, systematically secularized. The first purchase on the part of the town authorities on 2 November 1797 was the artistic wealth of the Jesuit church. Many monasteries were transformed into barracks and the great wealth of the libraries and archives was transferred to Paris or Brussels.

The *Reliquary of the Three Kings*, which had been put into safety in 1794 in the monastery of Weddinghausen near Arnsberg, was brought back to Cologne in 1803, even though it had been severely damaged.

In 1815, after the Congress of Vienna, Cologne was handed over to Prussia. It signalled the end of the French period after 21 years, and all that survived from it were certain words of French origin in the Cologne dialect. The name of the famous "4711" perfume dates back to that period. In 1795 the city was divided into four districts and houses were distinguished one from the other by progressive numbering; in this way, the house on the Glockengasse, which was subsequently the headquarters of the Mühlens family, was numbered 4711, and the eau de cologne manufactured there became famous throughout the world with the name "4711".

Cologne's strictly neutral policy managed to keep the city out of the wars of the 16th, 17th and 18th centuries, but it had lost importance and influence compared to cities in southern Germany which had developed in the meantime. The expulsion of the rich, powerful Geusen family in 1575, a few years after the foundation of the Cologne Stock Exchange (1553), had negative repercussions. The Archbishops, as Electors, had established their residence in Brühl and in Bonn; as a result, they were not allowed to enter the city as

Left page, above, the austere interior of St. Maria Himmelfahrt (1618-1627); below, the Perfume Museum in the Farina-Haus in front of the Town Hall, the oldest perfume factory in the world where, three hundred years ago, thanks to Giovanni Maria Farina, the glorious history of eau de Cologne began.

On this page, right, the celebrated *Kallendresser*, the curious little statue looking out from the top of a house over the Old Market, whose meaning has been variously interpreted in the course of time; below, an old photograph of the characteristic "Zur Brezel", one of the most striking Renaissance houses in the Alter Markt.

from 1288 without the Council's authorization. On the other hand, the city's bourgeois development was possible only on these conditions. This led to the creation of collections of books and works of art, some of which, however, had to be sold to the biggest English and Dutch collectors in order to meet more urgent expenses in the architectural field. As regards the bourgeois circle, one name suffices: Everhard Jabach, born in 1618, today remembered by the street near St. Peter and St. Cäcilien, whose considerable artistic wealth is housed at the Paris Louvre.

As examples of residential buildings in the Renaissance era, we can indicate here the houses of the Alten Markt, called "Zur Brezel" and "Zum Dorn", which with their five storeys reflect the wealth of those times. In the adjoining house, at number 24, the *Kallendresser,* Mataré's small figure in bronze, is at the same time a mockery of the unbearable hygienic situation of those decades.

The only important building that was erected in Cologne during the Thirty Years' War is the church of St. Mariä Himmelfahrt, built between 1618 and 1627, the only major example of a religious building in the Baroque style in Cologne. Destroyed during the last war, it has been rebuilt and brought back to its former glory together with the monastery.

Museum Ludwig

In 1976 Irene and Peter Ludwig decided to donate to the city of Cologne a collection of about 350 contemporary art works. By contract, the city authorities set about constructing the museum that would house the important and valuable collection, commissioning the project to the studio of architects Busmann & Habener. Opened in 1986, the sinuous building of 10,000 m^2, faced entirely in zinc and bricks, provoked a chorus of protests due to its very strong contrast with the adjacent cathedral.

The original project anticipated housing both the Ludwig collection and the Wallraf-Richartz Museum, but in 2001 the latter, renamed Wallraf-Richartz-Museum & Fondation Corboud, was moved to another venue. The project itself was modified to allow a less complicated access to the various sections. Two large stairways enable visitors to pass from one collection to the other: from the large entrance hall, one leads to the three floors of the permanent exhibition, while the other leads to the temporary exhibitions.

Represented in the Ludwig collection are the most important trends in modern art. It boasts the largest collection of Russian avant-garde in the

The Museum Ludwig, a short distance from the Cathedral, housed in a very modern building (below left, the south entrance), boasts a very rich collection Pop Art, Abstract and Surrealist art, as well as one of the largest Picasso collections in the world (above, his *Nu couché à l'oiseau* of 1968).

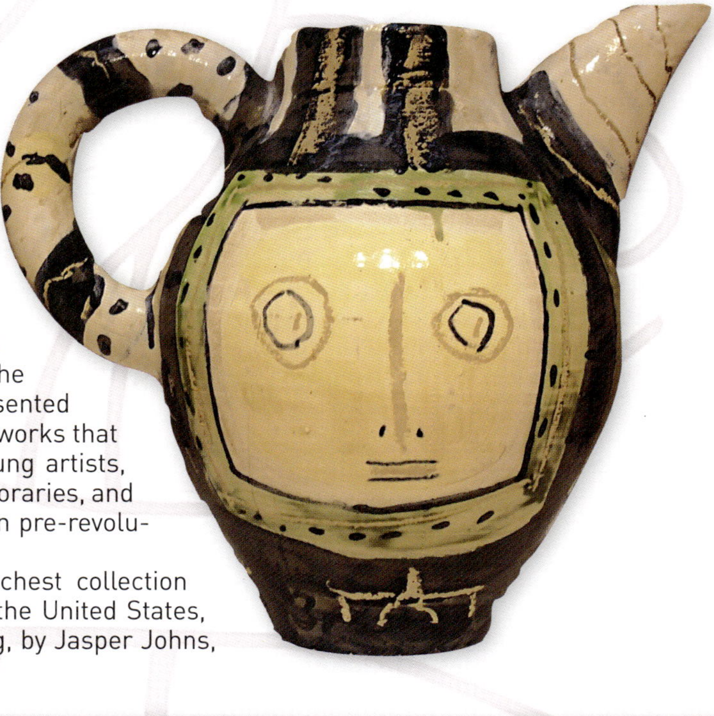

West, with over six hundred works dating from the period 1905-1935 (by artists like Natalia Goncharova, Michael Larionov, Alexandra Exter, Liubov Popova, 62 works by Casimir Malevich, Alexandr Rodchenko). Major examples of neo-Primitivism, Cubo-Futurism, Constructivism and the various tendencies of the period are abundantly represented in this superb exhibition, with works that express the energy of the young artists, inspired by European contemporaries, and the charged cultural climate in pre-revolutionary Russia.
Also exhibited here is the richest collection of American Pop Art outside the United States, with works, donated to Ludwig, by Jasper Johns,

Robert Rauschenberg, Andy Warhol, Roy Lichtenstein, James Rosenquist, Claes Oldenburg, George Segal and Tom Wesselmann – to name but a few – and splendid examples of American abstract painting, with Mark Rothko, Ellsworth Kelly, Morris Louis and Frank Stella. In the 1960s Pop Art brought art into daily life, transforming objects of everyday use into works of art, expressing concepts of protest and aversion to consumerism, and to cultural standardization, with a terminology and symbolism taken from advertising and the mass media. Displayed here are icons of American Pop Art, *M-Maybe* by Roy Lichtenstein, *Brillo Boxes* by Andy Warhol and *Res-*

Above, a view of the modern interior of the Museum Ludwig, with (right) an original hyper-realist sculpture, *Untitled* by John De Andrea.

taurant Window by George Segal. In 1994 and in 2001 the Ludwigs dedcided to donate to the museum their Picasso collection. Presently the museum possesses the third largest collection of Picassos in the world, with nine hundred works comprising paintings, sculpture and ceramics, and relating particularly to the last decades of the artist's production. The splendid *Arlequin, les mains croisées* ("Harlequin with Hands Folded"), of 1923, reproposes the theme of the circus dear to the artist. In his *Nu couché à l'oiseau*, of 1968, the artist portrays his second wife Jacqueline Rocque, lying naked with a dove in her hand, using an extraordinary perspective that shows her simultaneously from the front, the side and the back.

In 1946 the lawyer Josef Haubrich donated numerous masterpieces by Erich Heckel, Karl Schmidt-Rottluff, August Macke, Otto Müller, Otto Dix, Ernst Ludwig Kirchner and Marc Chagall. Later, works were acquired by Willi Baumeister, Max Beckmann, Alexej von Jawlensky, Paul Klee, Oskar Kokoschka, Henri Matisse and Ernst Wilhelm Nay.
The museum also houses an extremely important section dedicated to photography and a remarkable collection of graphic and video art.

More modern works of art at the Museum Ludwig: note in particular (above) the celebrated *Black Nana* by Niki de Saint Phalle (1968-1969).

From the Congress of Vienna to the Present Day

Under the influence of Prussian rigidity, the Rhine way of life did not change a great deal. In the decades after 1815 there was frenetic economic development, which also changed the city. The city walls had remained intact until 1881, that is, even after the Cathedral had been completed (1880). Only in 1881 was the first opening made in it. In 1822, the population numbered 56,000 inhabitants. In 1888 it suddenly increased, until in 1975, after the city reform, it surpassed the million mark. Today it is hard to believe that the walls facing the Rhine were opened only in 1891. The right bank of the Rhine was connected to the city by a bridge near Mulheim, and by a railway bridge near the Cathedral, called the "mousetrap". The Hohenzollern Bridge was built between 1907 and 1911; it is divided into two parts, one for the railway and one for cars. In 1906, the south bridge was built amid great difficulties.

The city's appearance after the First World War is closely associated with the name of the mayor Konrad Adenauer. During that period, the new bridge near Mulheim was built, the longest in Europe at the time. Adenauer

Images of modern Cologne, with the historic centre dominated by the huge Cathedral, the station, the Hohenzollern Bridge spanning the placid waters of the Rhine and, here above, the Roman-Germanic Museum.

bought the ground that stretched for 30 kilometres outside the walls and contained the strip of garden inside it, 7 kilometres long. Today these gardens are an integral part of the city; in the middle of them stands the stadium, built between 1921 and 1923, modernized in the years 1973-1975, totally renovated in 2004 and surrounded by other sports buildings.
Ninety per cent of the city's buildings were destroyed during the Second World War, and the population decreased to 40,000 inhabitants. But it soon picked up again: the first sign of recovery was the celebration held at the Cathedral in 1948. In 1949, the inhabitants of Cologne had the determination to revive an old tradition, dating back to 1823, that of the *Carnival parade*. When the procession passed in front of the Gürzenich building, with its reception hall in ruins, the prince got out of his car, brandished a shovel, and declared that the reconstruction of the city was the duty of all its townsfolk.
The "National Garden Exhibition", held in 1957, allowed visitors from faraway to see that Cologne, even though it protected its ancient monuments and traditional areas, had become a modern city where, thanks to the earthmoving and building carried out in the previous decades, history and the present day could coexist in extraordinary harmony.
If one observes a picture of Cologne in 1850, seen from the Rhine, one gets the impression of being in the Middle Ages: the walls, ships, men, everything would suggest that our own age is centuries away. A link with the late 19th century is given by the numerous romantic fountains of Albermann and others, like the one in front of St. Georg of 1894, Werth's fountain at the Alter Markt of 1884, the "Gnomes Fountain" near the Cathedral, and many others built since then up to the present day, showing the pleasure derived by the inhabitants of Cologne in plays of water and peace of mind. It is also worth mentioning the "Fountain of Petrus" behind the Cathedral, the Roman fountain gushing water along the road to the Shipyard, and Mataré's small "Pigeon Fountain" in which the Cathedral spires are reflected.
In Cologne, to find past together with the present in works of art, all one has to do is walk the streets and look around. The great destruction during the last war and the subsequent reconstructions brought to light numerous remains from the past, which were left alongside modern buildings and now line the streets. Undoubtedly the museums, with their precious neatly classified treasures, play an important role in getting to know, and growing to love, Cologne. The **Roman-Germanic Museum,** on the south

side of the Cathedral, introduces us to Cologne's Roman past. The museum was built where the *Dionysus Mosaic*, belonging to a Roman villa, was discovered in 1941 during the building of an air-raid bunker. A nearby house, located at no. 2 Roncalli square, for a long time housed the **Diocesan Museum** (since 2007 incorporated into the **Kolumba**), exhibiting works of art mainly belonging to the Cathedral, from Heriman's *Crucifix* to Stephan Lochner's *Madonna of the Violet*. The site of the Roman Praetorium, discovered under the Town Hall, is the starting point for the discovery of Roman Cologne.

Not far away is the **Museum Ludwig**, with its unmistakable building specially constructed between the Cathedral and the Rhine, and, proceeding beyond the Town Hall, the **Wallraf-Richartz Museum**, with its rich collections exhibited in the modern building which opened in 2001.

Lovers of exotic art will find interesting pieces, covering a period of two thousand years, in the **Museum of Asiatic Art**, at the Aachener Weiher, and in the **Rautenstrauch Joest Museum**, with its rich collections of extraordinary ethnological value. Special mention must also be made of the **Schnütgen Museum** inside the Romanesque Cäcilienkirche; here about 1800 works of art coming from churches in the city that were by then secularized, were collected by Alexander Schnütgen (1843-1918), cathedral capitular and art-lover. In 1906 the collection was donated to the city of Cologne.

The old **Opera House** was completely destroyed during the war. The new one, according to the city's renovation project, was built along the north-south axis, together with the Offenbachplatz, near the large complexes of West German Radio, which represented a crucial area in the new urban layout. This unusual, complex building, completed in 1957 by Wilhelm Riphahn, was dubbed with the most outlandish names (such as that of Ghandi), by the inhabitants of Cologne who are always ready for a joke. The **Playhouse**, built in 1960-1962, is much simpler and less striking. The north side of the square is graced by a fountain, flowers and benches, from where one can admire the spires of the Csathedral.

From the time of the Hanseatic League, Cologne has retained its importance as a traffic junction and trade centre, a fact confirmed by its eight bridges over the Rhine. Cologne, the country's third internal port, holds, the record for tourist movement in Germany.

The view of the Rhine is characterized by large, white passenger ships, which travel up and down the most beautiful stretch of the river between Cologne and Mainz.

The **Stock Exchange**, founded in Cologne in 1553, and fifth in the world, is still very important today. In recent years, moreover, Cologne has become famous all over the world for its car production and oil refineries. The approximately 130,000 employees who work in industry can be added to the numerous employees in the tertiary sector (particularly insurance and the media), making Cologne and its environs a catchment basin with 2,500,000-3,000,000 inhabitants.

The interesting Wallraf-Richartz Museum, one of the most important art galleries in the whole of Germany, is noteworthy for its modern, functional building, constructed in 2001 to designs by the architect Oswald Mathias Ungers.

An image of Cologne lying along the course of the Rhine, over which the Prussian Malakoffturm with its battlemented tower seems still to keep watch. Recognizable in the background is the majestic profile of the Cathedral and the tower of the church of Great St. Martin.

Visitors to the **Fair** held in front of the cathedral, on the right bank of the Rhine, get an excellent impression of the city. Built in 1922-24 by H. Verbeek and by Pieper, the building of the Fair, the heart of an extremely modern exhibition centre, has housed numerous national and international exhibitions, as well as congresses. Sports events are also held there. Visitors who wish to stroll in the open air find plenty of green space in the nearby **Rheinpark,** in 2007 declared the most beautiful park in Germany.

Cologne's inhabitants are as passionate about music as they are of the figurative arts. The most outstanding orchestras are those of the Gürzenich and the Opera, which contribute to spreading Cologne's fame as a city of music. The most important places for the culture and study of music are the University and the Music Academy. Interest in music has been stimulated by the organization of choirs and orchestras in schools, and thanks to the contribution of parish churches to church music, which has reached a very high standard in Cologne.

Other tourist attractions, on the left bank of the Rhine, are **Flora**, the city's botanical garden, and the **Zoo**, which are all close to one another; a much-frequented *cableway* connects them to the large Rheinpark on the right bank of the river. The exotic buildings for animals inside the zoo reflect the style in fashion in about 1860 when they were built. One can still recognize the original style in the Flora gardens too, despite the renovations in 1955-1956.

Another point of interest is the **stadium** with its sports installations situated within the green belt at Müngersdorf. Built in 1923, the stadium has been enlarged several times; in 1973-1975 the main arena was built, whose covered stands accommodated 70,000 spectators. In anticipation of the World Cup in 2006 the stadium was completely rebuilt between 2001 and 2004 and took the name **RheinEnergieStadion**; today it has a capacity of over 50,000 spectators.

With regard to the city's main recreational areas, mention must be made of the green belt, where the **University** stands and where the inhabitants of Cologne built a hill with the rubble of buildings de-

stroyed during the war, appropriately named "Mount Clamott". In this area stands the television tower, almost 250 metres high, called "Colonius", providing a panoramic view of the city, the industrial area and the extensive area of lignite deposits to the west. In the 20th century the man who made history in Cologne more than anyone else is Konrad Adenauer (1876-1967). Born in Cologne, he graduated in law; in 1906, he became a city councillor and from 1917 to 1933 he was mayor of the city. Under his administration, Cologne gradually picked up again after the First World War. In 1919, the old University was rebuilt. With the construction of the exhibition area in 1924, the city increased its economic resources and reached European standards with the great "Millenary Exhibition of the Rhineland". Adenauer was not only responsible for the construction of the stadium but also for the so-called green rings, two ring roads — one inside and one outside the city centre characterized by a series of recreational and sports installations and by open spaces made into public parks.

A panoramic view of modern Cologne, with its industries and green surroundings. Towering above it all is the unmistakable Telekom-Turm, the tower also known familiarly as "Colonius".

Konrad Adenauer (1876-1967), one of the most important politicians of post-war Germany, was previously the city's mayor; he had a major role in Cologne's reconstruction after the First World War.

His initiatives, such as the setting up of new industries and the construction of the port of Niehler, aimed above all at economic progress. The old-age homes of Riehler are eloquent proof of the attention he paid to the problems of the aged and infirm. The construction of the new university was also begun while he was in office in 1929, and completed in 1934. By incorporating many of the city's suburbs in the city territory, Adenauer turned Cologne into a fully-fledged metropolis, despite inflation and the economic depression. With the advent of the Third Reich in 1933, he was removed from office and two years later expelled from the city. After the war, when re-elected mayor, he immediately dealt with the urgent problems of the population and the far-sighted project for the reconstruction of the city, 70% of which had been destroyed. He was once again dismissed from office by members of the occupying British army in 1945.

The real career of the then seventy-year old politician started in 1946. As president of the Christian Democratic Union and president of the Parliamentary Council, his participation was decisive in the drawing-up of the Constitution of the West German Republic, of which he was the first Chancellor from 1949 to 1963.

He was deeply attached to Cologne until he died. An unprecedented funeral procession accompanied his coffin from the cathedral to the ship that transported it to Rhondorf, where he was then buried. The road along the Rhine in front of the exhibition area was called Konrad-Adenauer-Ufer.

In talking about Cologne, the Carnival immediately comes to mind. In fact, the so-called "mad days" form an integral part of city life involving even schools, offices and companies. The Carnival can be traced back to an old pagan tradition, according to which during some days of the year one lives illogically: everyone has the right to express his opinion, at least once a year – students to teachers, apprentices to masters and employees to employers – and everyone can play the role he likes.

As mentioned previously, the two banks of the Rhine are presently connected by eight bridges. Whereas at one time in Cologne it was said that behind Deutz lay Asia, nowadays the two parts of the city situated on either side of the river, which is 400 metres wide at this point, create a single urban centre. The bridges painted green that cross them bring to mind old songs in which the river was called the "green Rhine". It was the Emperor Constantine who built the first bridge, which no longer exists. Some old townsfolk still recall the old bridge of boats. It was in 1859 that the city's first stone bridge was built; it susbsequently became the **Hohenzollernbrücke** and at present is crossed by about 1400 trains every day. Up until the First World War, three stable bridges existed on the Rhine. In 1927-1928, while Konrad Adenauer was in office, the **Mülheimer Brücke** was completed; 708 metres long, it was the longest suspension bridge at the time. The **Rodenkirchener Bridge** was built in 1941. After the war, all destroyed bridges were

rebuilt alongside other new ones: the **Severinsbrücke** in 1959, the **Merkenicher Autobahnbrücke** in 1965 and the **Zoobrücke** in 1966. An interesting feature is the structure of the Severinsbrücke, which is 691 metres long and whose cables all start from a triangular, assymetric pylon. Each of the bridges over the Rhine stands out on account of one of its aesthetic or structural characteristics; it is therefore worth taking a stroll in the gardens along the river and especially in the splendid Rheinpark, near the exhibition area, to get a close-up of them. Despite all the modern bridges, the townsfolk of Cologne still have fond memories of the "Mülheimer Böötchen", or boat of Mülheim, and even today cross the Rhine on the small "Strolch" to go to the Fair.

Modern churches also play an important role in the field of renovation and reconstruction of the city. The need for new buildings was not only the result of damage caused by war but also of the progressive decentralization of the built-up area. An entire generation of important builders and artists was available for this task. Some names were already well-known, such as Karl Band, Wilhelm Riphahn, etc. An example of modern architecture is provided by St. Maria Königin in Marienburg, constructed by the famous modern architect, Dominikus Böhm at the end of his career, and the Kirche Christi Auferstehung (Resurrection of Christ), in Melaten, designed by his son Gottfried in 1967-1970.

Dominikus Böhm is considered one of the exponents of avant-garde of new religious architecture. In 1931, he designed the **church of St. Engelbert** at Köln-Riehl, near to the Zoo and to the Flora; it has a central plan and is built in concrete. The basic idea was that of a church intended as a curtain of God. This concept was revived by the architect later on in 1953-1954 at Marienburg, where on the edge of the Südpark he built the church of his own parish, **Maria Königin**. This unusual construction, built in pumice-stone concrete covered in brick, blends in perfectly amid the centuries-old trees in the area. The south side, consisting of a single glass wall, provides light for the interior. Through the symbols of the Loretan litanies, the maestro created an environment that gives the impression of the cloak of the Queen of Heaven. The four red columns supporting the roof underline the concept of the curtain of God. A 15th-century *statue of the Virgin Mary*, to whom the church is dedicated, stands above the altar. The tabernacle and baptismal font, built with magnificent enamels, are the work of Hanns Rheindorf. One gains access to the church's interior from the luminous rotonda of the baptistery.

With this late work, the great architect of modern churches, Dominikus Böhm, leaves profound evidence of his faith to future generations.

His message was carried on in particular by his son Gottfried, who designed numerous churches, including the **church of the Resurrection of Christ** at Melaten. Built in 1967-1970, it is one of the most recent churches in Cologne and blends perfectly into its green surroundings between Danteweg and Clarenbachstraße.

The modern building of Lufthansa, the principal German aviation company and only one of the many important world-renowned companies to have chosen Cologne as the location for its headquarters.

Cardinal Josef Frings was undoubtedly one of the most eminent and popular figures in Cologne in the 20th century. He became archbishop on 1 May 1942 and played a major role in tackling the devastation inflicted on the city by the Second World War. He died on 17 December 1978 at the age of 91 and was buried in the archbishop's crypt of Cologne Cathedral.

The massive brick construction, with sober interior decoration, is very striking for its markedly vertical thrust. The multi-coloured, assymetrical windows and the cross, inviting the congregation to look upwards, are a reminder that through the Resurrection of Jesus all men are called upon to live in love of God.
Nor must one forget the name of the architect and modern rebuilder of the Cathedral, W. Weyres and his successors for the diocese: W. Schlombs, F. Schaller, J. Schürmann and R. Schwarz. Among the interior decorators are Elmar Hillebrand, Hanns Rheindorf, Peter Hecker, Ludwig Gies, Georg Meistermann, and others.
Also memorable in the history of Cologne is the figure of the extremely popular Cardinal Josef Frings, who after the war had to rebuild 300 churches. Innumerable also the townsfolk who helped him to save the Cathedral and other churches, spending the nights of the bombardments of the Second World War in the floors of the churches of Cologne ready to extinguish any fires. Without mentioning the thousands of women who after the war had to start again from scratch, removing the rubble from the city with their bare hands.
What has been written up to now can only give an idea of Cologne's very rich history, a city that deserves to be known. In Germany, there are very few cities in which the past blends in with the present as it does here. The war, by destroying almost the entire city, created many open spaces. And even today the past comes out of the ruins. Fortunately surviving the two World Wars without any damage was the largest communal archive in Germany. What brought it to the ground, in 2009, were the works and underground excavations for the new underground railway. The reconstruction of the **Stadtarchiv** is now planned for 2014, while the restoration and recovery of the historical material, 90% of which was seriously damaged, should be completed only by 2040. And in the meantime the city continues to adapt to the requirements of modern society and the modern economy. Today, for example, Cologne has become one of the most important cities for German television, with the setting up of the RTL and WDR studios. It is also a major centre for automobile manufacturing, with the Ford and Toyota plants and the important surrounding area.
In 2012 one of the largest **mosques** in Germany was opened on the Venloer Straße, another milestone of the architecture of the third millennium of this city.
The open space created by the bombing of the last war has been used essentially to meet the requirements of modern life, albeit with constant respect for the legacies of the past. With the result that in the throbbing metropolis ancient Cologne stays alive. During the Carnival season, it plays and laughs at itself in the comical personifications of Tünnes and Schäl, and sings sentimental love songs for its country, even during the years of evacuation and destruction.
In 1531 Anton Woensam entitled his famous work *De sacra et civili magnitudine Coloniae*. These pages have also wanted to tell the story of the "Grandeur of sacred, civilized Cologne".

Sports and Olympic Museum

In the northern area of the Rheinauhafen, near the Chocolate Museum, is the Sports and Olympic Museum, occupying former warehouses of the old customs of the port of Rheinau. Opened in 1999, it is one of the most modern museums in Cologne, a blend of tradition, innovation and technology. In an exhibition area covering approximately 2000 m^2, the history of sports and their evolution through the centuries – through objects, equipment, anecdotes and legends linked to the various disciplines – is recounted in a totally innovative and interactive way. Arranged on two floors, the first dedicated to the permanent exhibition, the second reserved for temporary exhibitions and special events, the museum boasts a rich collection made up of about one hundred thousand items ranging from clothes, sports and games equipment, medals, documents, sports prizes, art manifestos, offering visitors the opportunity to make a veritable journey through time. The story begins thousands of years ago, on an athletics field in ancient Greece, to

then continue with the most important sporting events in history in a time sequence divided up over 80 m in length. The evolution of gymnastics and sport particularly in Germany and England in the 19th century, up to modern professional sports and the great athletes of today. There are numerous curiosities and "symbolic" objects on display here, including a tennis racket smashed to pieces with his own hands by Boris Becker and the shoes

of the Formula 1 champion Michael Schumacher.
A large area is given over to the Olympic Games of Berlin in 1936 and those of Munich in 1972.
In some sections visitors can actually get a taste of the various disciplines, like in the perfectly reconstructed boxing ring, or in the wind gallery where the various speeds at the Tour de France are simulated.
On the roof of the museum is a sports field has been reconstructed, where you can play football, basketball or tennis, and enjoy magnificent views of the city.

The Chocolate Museum

In 1993 the businessman Hans Imhoff founded the Chocolate Museum at the northern tip of the Rheinauhafen, the area of the city's trading port in medieval times. In March 2006 Lindt & Sprüngli began a collaboration with the museum, replacing the Stollwerck chocolate company, owned by the founder. In a building constructed in the form of a ship, built entirely of steel and glass, the three thousand year history of the precious food is recounted in an exhibition arranged on three floors.

The first part of the museum is occupied by a glasshouse covering an area of 100 m^2, 10 m in height, containing a reconstruction of the vegetation of Amazzonia. In a humid tropical environment, together with the plants of vanilla, coffee and banana, we find *Theobroma cacao*, from which the Aztecs obtained what they considered to be the "food of the gods". The processing starts with the extremely bitter cocoa pod: inside the museum, in real time, it is possible to follow the course of its transformation, through special machines, until it finally becomes paper-wrapped and boxed-up chocolate confectionery. Every day 400

Below, an image of the very modern building in steel and glass housing the Chocolate Museum, on the banks of the Rhine, a short distance from the city's historic centre and next to the Sports and Olympic Museum. Left, the famous and enormously popular Chocolate Fountain.

kg of chocolate are produced in the factory, in bars, individual sweets, and in all shapes and sizes.
The second floor is given over to the history of chocolate: prized since the time of its origins, venerated as a sacred food in central America,

it was a luxury item in Europe too, when it arrived here in the 18th century and refined sets of china and precious chocolate bowls were made to savour the exhilerating drink.
The third floor is devoted to advertising, vending machines, packaging, and everything representing the image of chocolate. From 1926, when it was advertised as an energy food, to the advertisements of the 1970s, which were almost like short films.
For the delight of children, and temptable adults too of course, inside the museum is a large golden fountain gushing 200 litres of flavoured liquid lukewarm chocolate, ... which it is of course possible to taste by dipping in a wafer!

"D'R KÖLSCHE FASTELOVEND" COLOGNE CARNIVAL

The Rhineland Carnival is based on the Roman festival of Saturnalia, which in the "Colonia Claudia Ara Agrippinensium" was celebrated, as in ancient Rome, from 17 to 19 December. The word "Carnival" would appear to derive from "carrus navalis", a float in the form of a ship that was used in this Roman colony during festivities. It is for this reason that one could say that the Carnival may have originated in Cologne! In the 5th century, to adapt these pagan rites to the Catholic liturgy, the festivity changed from being a winter festival to the *Fastabend*, an evening of fasting in Lent. The word "Fastelovend" for the Cologne Carnival also comes from this word. The masks, hubbub and merrymaking of this festival, today just as two thousand years ago, still have the same purpose: to scare off and banish winter demons! In the Middle Ages the Church tried to ban the festivities before Lent, or at least to instil them with a more religious tone, but their derivation from the Saturnalia, which also provided for a total reversal of the social order (servants became masters for one day) continued to prevail. Only in the 19th century did the Carnival begin to take on its present form, adopting the usages of the Italian Carnival with processions of musical bands and performers. Craftsmen and traders' guilds had increasing power and began to organize the festival, which even today is largely supervised by these unions. On the Thursday the The Women's Carnival ("Wieverfastelovend") started to be established: on that day women took over control of the city (another sign of the reversal of roles dictated by the Saturnalia), and the day was given over to celebrations that continued until Rose Monday. In 1794, under French rule, the Carnival was banned; it therefore began to be celebrated secretly, and consequently it became politicized. Following the expulsion of the French by the Prussians in 1815, the Carnival degraded into an increasingly vulgar celebration. Risking a ban even by the Prussian authorities, the bourgeoisie resumed their supervision of the carnival's organization and brought it back to being a festival halfway between religion and

popular cult. To give the Carnival greater sobriety the hero "Carnival" and his eternal bride "Venetia" were invented, who "reigned" over the city during the festivities, thus putting an end to the excessive extravagance and vulgarity. The customs and traditions of the modern Carnival reflect many of these historical elements.
The organizational part of the Carnival begins on 11 November, at 11 minutes past 11. The "street" Carnival, on the other hand, which takes place in the week before Ash Wednesday, starts on the Thursday at 11 minutes past 11 with the Women's Day. In the City Hall the mayor consigns command of the city to the three sovereigns of the Carnival: the prince, the knave, representing the city's defensive power, and the virgin, the symbol of Cologne, figures who, with the passing of time, have replaced "Carnival" and "Venetia" and who in their turn now direct the Carnival. A parade, accompanied by dancing and music, departs from the Severinstor and reaches the Alter Markt, where the monument to Jan von Werth stands. Males, beware! Women have permission to behave badly! They may kiss whoever passes their way and carry a pair of scissors with them, to cut... the ends of men's ties!
Rose Monday was originally a Catholic festival. On that day the Pope consecrated a rose that was then carried in procession through the streets of Rome. Today, Rose Monday ("Rusemondach") is the most important moment of the Carnival. This is the day of the grand procession of allegorical floats, inspired by great topical contemporary themes represented in tongue-in-cheek fashion. The parade passes through the city streets, attracting hundreds of thousands of tourists every year. The crowd are showered with flowers and sweets ("Strüssjer un Kamelle") thrown from the floats. Kisses can be given to policemen (and policewomen!), who on these special days are "easy prey". Kisses are requested with the cry "bützjer" (kisses)... for those who want them! Those looking for a "quieter" parade are advised to follow that of the schools and neighbourhoods ("Schull- un Veedelszöch"), on Carnival Sunday, on the same route as the "grown-ups" with the participation of lots of children.
On Ash Wednesday the city returns to "normal", or, as a popular song of the Cologne Carnival goes: "Am Aschermittwoch ist alles vorbei" ("Everything's over on Ash Wednesday").
Kölle Alaaf!

Index